CW00924587

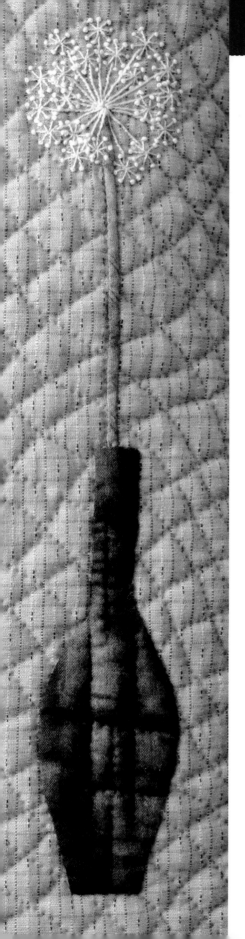

Notes from the Publisher

Welcome to a glimpse into the world of international quilting. At Stitch Publications our wish is for you to be able to explore beyond the boundaries of the country you live in to experience and see what other fiber artists are doing.

In many countries, rather than learning from various books, quilters study under a single master, spending years progressing from simple techniques to the extremely difficult. Intricate designs are celebrated and sewing and quilting by hand is honored and as such, hand quilting is the typical method used to quilt.

This book was written in its original language, Japanese, by a master quilter, Yoko Saito. We have done our best to make the directions for each project easy to understand if you have some level of quilting experience, while maintaining the appearance and intent of the original author and publisher.

We hope the beautifully designed handmade items in this book inspire and encourage you to make them for yourself.

- Important Tips Before You Begin -

The following facts might suggest that intermediate or advanced quilters will be more comfortable working on these projects.

- Techniques -

Beyond the two Step-by-Step lessons (in pictures), Ms. Saito does not go into detailed descriptions of specific quilting or sewing methods for each project. She assumes that the creator is familiar with sewing, quilting and bag-making techniques to some degree and thus relies heavily on the creator's ability to figure out the directions that are not specifically written out. It is advisable to read through and understand each project's direction page from beginning to end, including finding the corresponding patterns on the included pattern sheets before beginning.

- Measurements -

The original designs were created using the metric system for dimensions. In order to assist you, we have included the imperial system measurements in brackets. However, please note that samples that appear in the book were created and tested using the metric system. Thus, you will find that if you use the imperial measurements to make the projects, the items you make will not be exactly the same size as when using the metric measurements.

- Patterns/Templates -

Full pattern information for each project appears in several different ways: a) in the materials list b) in the illustrations and captions c) in the pattern sheet insert. One must read through all the instructions carefully to understand what size to cut the fabric and related materials, including instructions for each project relating to seam allowances.

- Notions/Accessories -

Some of the projects in this book will call for a variety of accessories such as zippers, handles, and hardware. While the originals were made with items from Japan, most if not all of the accessories seen have comparable items or are available around the world. However, some of the accessories are available through Yoko Saito's quilt shop in Japan. See the copyright page for further information.

Stitch Publications, 2014

Yoko Saito's

Floral Bouquet Quilts

Introduction

When I design quilts, the selection of fabrics is critical to my process. Not only do the colors that I use set the overall feeling of the quilt, but the background fabric or fabric that I choose to use more than others, can significantly alter the impression of the finished product. But that is what is so much fun about quilting, isn't it? I have used an assortment of fabrics for the various projects in this book.

The Floral Bouquet Wall Quilt includes both traditional appliqué and a three-dimensional aspect to the design that make it a signature piece when part of a room decor. Although not three-dimensional, I also particularly like the Earthenware Wall Quilt. Each of the vessels is unique. I think that it would be fun for you to appliqué flowers of your choice to fill the vases.

The quilts and projects in this book are ones that I created knowing that I would want to make and use each one myself. They are all practical for daily living. I hope that you take pleasure in making them and using them, as all quilted items are made to be enjoyed to the greatest extent.

Yoko Saito

2

Contents

Spring Tulip Bag

instructions p. *54*

Earthenware Wall Quilt

instructions p. *66*

*Floral Bouquet
Wall Quilt*

instructions p. *68*

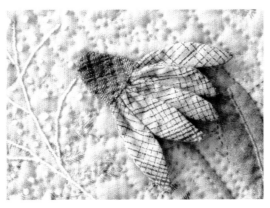

Garden Bounty
Placemats

instructions p. *65*

Garden Girl
Water Bottle Holder

instructions p. *70*

13

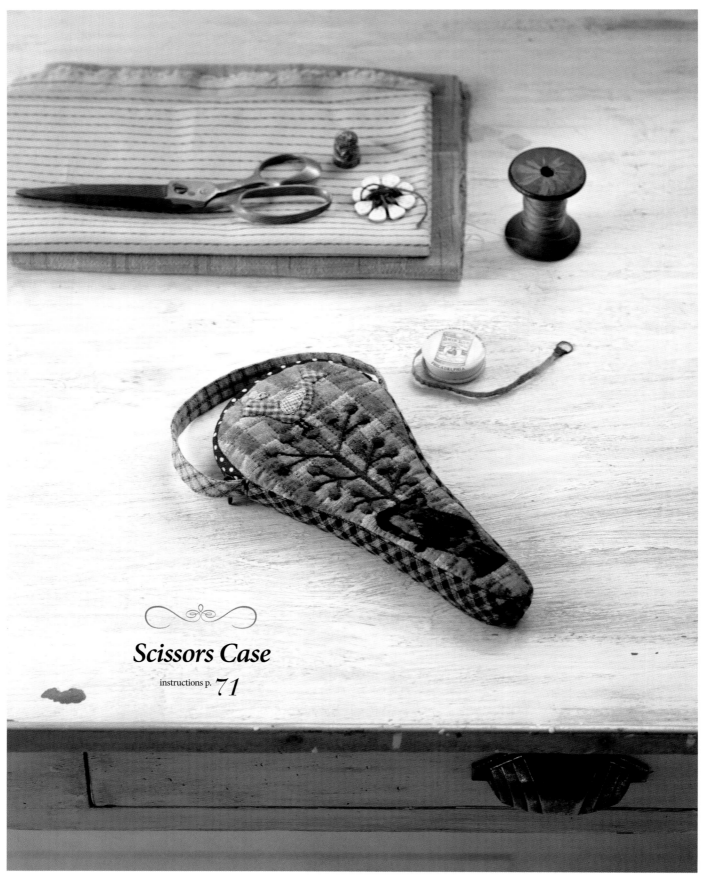

Scissors Case

instructions p. *71*

Rose Pouch

instructions p. 74

Wheelbarrow Pouch

instructions p. 75

16

Mini Card Holders

instructions p. 72

B

A

Watering Can Notebook Cover

instructions p. *76*

Queen Anne's Lace Bag

instructions p. 77

Floral Display Bag

instructions p. *78*

Songbird Mini Tote

instructions p. *80*

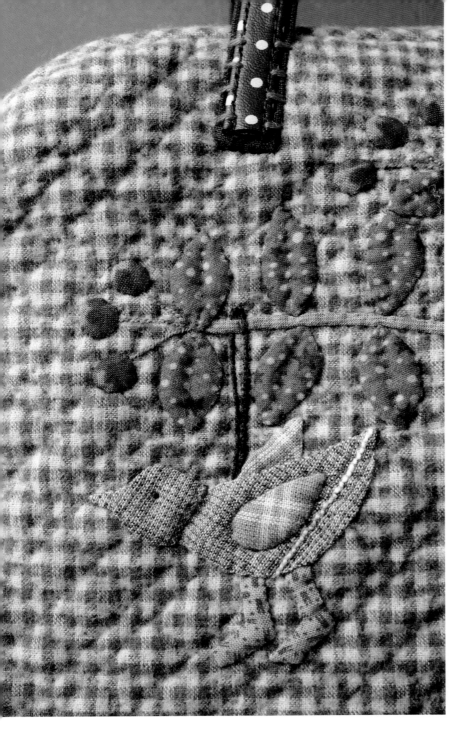

Bunny Bag

instructions p. *82*

Flowers, Birds & Butterflies
Wall Hanging

instructions p. *88*

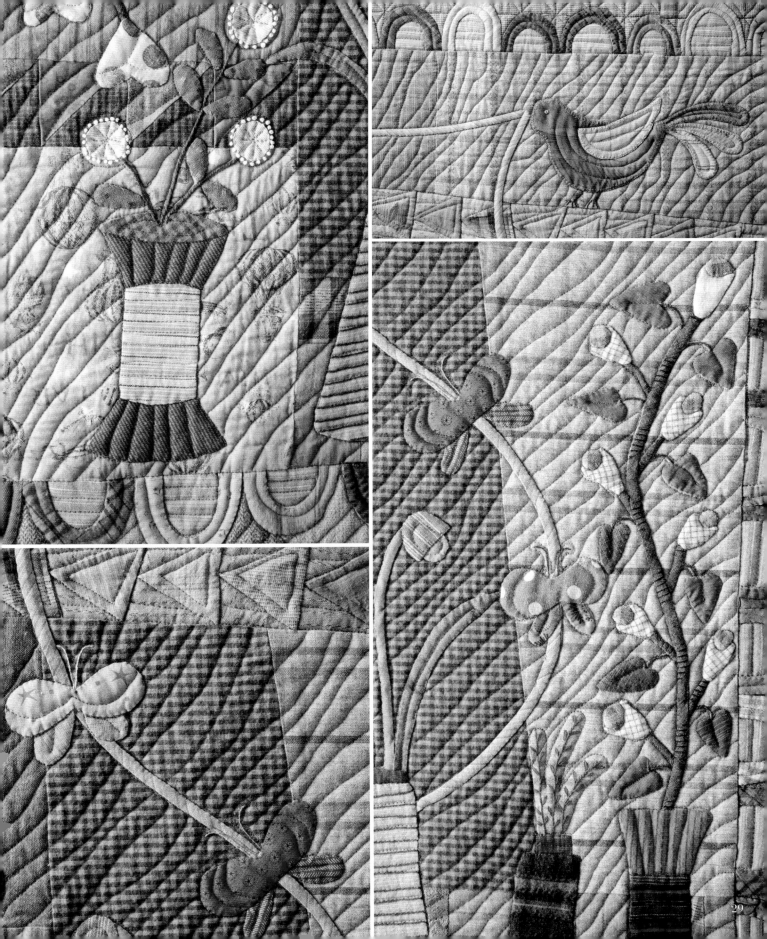

Floral Bucket

instructions p. *84*

Tulip Sewing Basket

instructions p. *102*

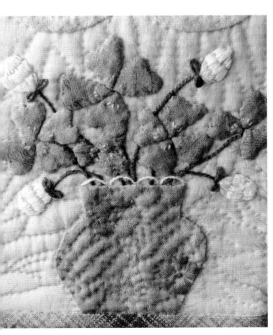

33

Floral Folk Art
Sewing Case

instructions p. *86*

35

Blossom Book Bag

instructions p. *89*

Little Bird Book Cover

instructions p. *93*

Botanical Cushion Cover

instructions p. *92*

Daisy Drawstring Bag

instructions p. *90*

41

Modern Floral Pouch

instructions p. *94*

Pomegranate Shoulder Bag

instructions p. *96*

Cosmos Pouch

instructions p. *98*

White Flower Tea Cozy

instructions p. *100*

Appliquéd Eco-Bag

instructions p. *104*

Floral Bird Tote

instructions p. *105*

*Vases of Flowers
Wall Quilt*

instructions p. *106*

Essential Quilting Notions & Tools

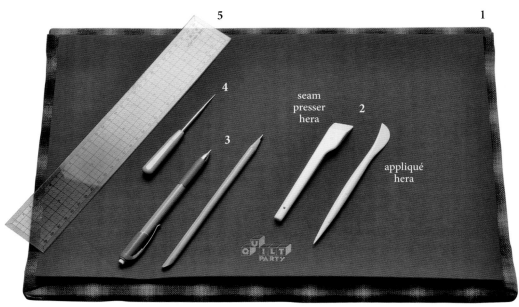

1. Non-Slip Board - The non-slip surface board is used when marking fabric or when using the fabric pressing tool to turn under the seam allowances. The soft side backed with batting and fabric can be used as a mini ironing surface.

2. Seam Pressing Tools - Used to press seam allowances down in lieu of ironing when working with appliqué pieces. (Finger Presser, Hera Markers).

3. Pencils • Chalk Pencils - used for copying patterns or marking quilting lines. If you use a pencil to mark quilting lines, use one with soft lead. The lines won't always disappear, so do not use for marking quilting lines.

4. Awl - To mark points when transferring and drawing patterns. Also useful for turning under seam allowances.

5. Rulers - Used to trace straight lines when transferring patterns. Rulers with markings made for quilters are useful.

6. Scissors - They will last longer if each pair is used for specific things, such as for paper, fabric or thread.

A - A pair specifically for fabric.
B - A pair specifically for thread.
C - A pair specifically for paper/patterns.

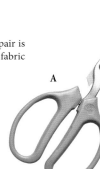
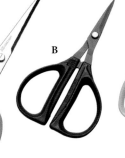

8. Thread

I - Quilting Thread - A coated, durable thread used for hand-quilting that is slightly thicker.
J - Sewing Thread - Used for piecing or stitching; appropriate for either hand sewing or machine sewing.
K - Basting Thread - Used for basting.

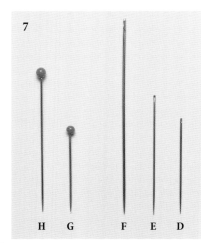

7. Pins and Needles

D - Quilting Betweens - A short needle approximately 2.5 cm [1"] long used specifically for quilting.
E - Appliqué Needles - A long thin needle approximately 3 cm [1¼"] long, used for piecing and appliqué.
F - Basting Needles - A long needle used for basting.
G - Appliqué Pins - It is easiest to use ones that are very fine and have small heads.
H - Piecing Pins - Slightly longer and useful for piecing fabrics together.

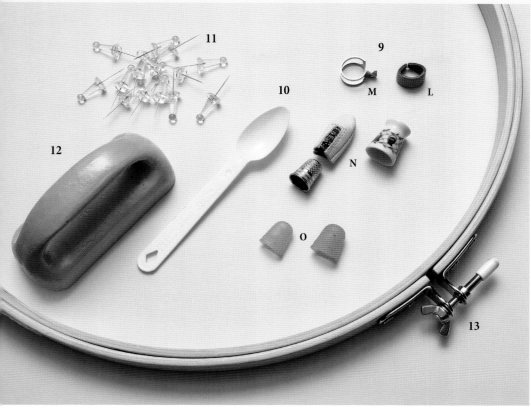

9. Thimbles

L - Leather ring - used while doing piecework.

M - Ring Cutter - Conveniently worn on your left (or right) thumb and used for cutting threads as you are working.

N - Metal or Porcelain Thimble - Used to push needle through cloth when quilting. Leather Thimble - slip this over a metal thimble on your middle finger as you work to keep work from slipping.

O - Rubber Thimbles
Wear on your right index finger during quilting or appliqué to help grab the needle and reduce slippage.

10. Spoon - Often used when pin basting a quilt. Safety pins are easy to use for this method.

11. Push Pins - Useful to keep layers from shifting when getting ready to baste quilting sandwich. The longer the pin, the better.

12. Weights (paperweight, beanbag, etc.) - Used to weigh down a small quilt when quilting.

13. Quilting Hoop - Used to hold quilt sandwich during quilting. It can also be used as a makeshift light table by holding up to window to transfer a pattern onto the fabric.

14. Tube Turners
Used to turn fabric tubes right side out or for making piping cord.

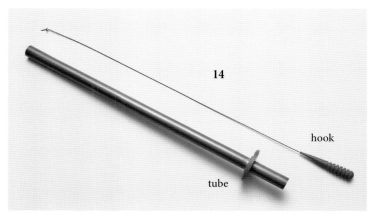

🌿 Other notions and tools might be necessary:
Hoops (quilting), quilt stand (used when quilting large projects), heavyweight paper (for templates/patterns), tracing paper, light table, cellophane tape, iron, spray adhesive.

🍂 **Spring Tulip Bag** ⊠ The full-size template/pattern can be found on Side A of the pattern sheet inserts.

🍂 **Finished measurements**
26 × 28 cm [10¼" × 11"] (bag opening) × 9 cm [3½"](gusset)

Contrasting thread has been used in the photos for instructional purposes.

Dimensional Diagram

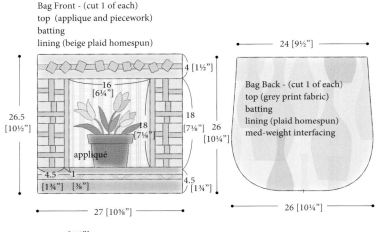

Bag Front - (cut 1 of each)
top (applique and piecework)
batting
lining (beige plaid homespun)

26.5 [10½"]

4 [1½"]

16 [6¼"]

18 [7⅛"]

18 [7⅛"]

appliqué

4.5 [1¾"]   1 [⅜"]

4.5 [1¾"]

27 [10⅝"]

24 [9½"]

Bag Back - (cut 1 of each)
top (grey print fabric)
batting
lining (plaid homespun)
med-weight interfacing

26 [10¼"]

26 [10¼"]

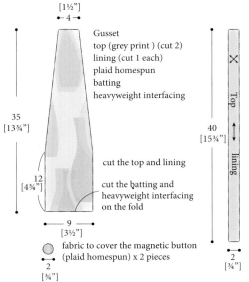

[1½"]
4

Gusset
top (grey print) (cut 2)
lining (cut 1 each)
plaid homespun
batting
heavyweight interfacing

35 [13¾"]

12 [4¾"]

cut the top and lining

cut the batting and
heavyweight interfacing
on the fold

9 [3½"]

fabric to cover the magnetic button
(plaid homespun) x 2 pieces

2 [¾"]

Handle (cut 2 of each)
top (cut 1 each)
blue-grey and brown prints
lining (green print)
med-weight interfacing

× Top ↕ lining

40 [15¾"]

2 [¾"]

* Cut all interfacing without seam
allowances.
Add a seam allowance of 3 cm
[1¼"] to the bag front, bag back,
gusset batting, and lining, and
0.7 cm [¼"] for all other pieces.

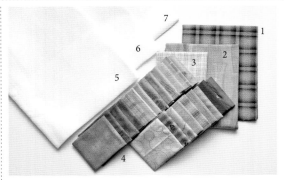

7
1
6
2
3
5
4

🍂 **Materials**
1 Plaid homespun - 110 × 50 cm [43¼" × 19¾"]
(bag lining, gusset lining, fabric to cover magnetic buttons,
bias binding for the bag opening)
2 Grey print - 50 × 50 cm [19¾" × 19¾"]
(bag back top, gusset top, handle lining)
3 Beige plaid homespun - 20 × 18 cm [7⅞" × 7⅛"]
(appliqué background fabric)
4 Assorted fat quarters or scraps - 20 kinds (as required for
appliqué and piecing); Blue-gray print/brown print -
35 × 35 cm [13¾" × 13¾"] each (handle top)
5 Batting - 50 × 80 cm [19¾" × 31½"]
6 Medium-weight interfacing: 30 × 40 cm [11¾" × 15¾"]
(bag back, handle)
7 Heavyweight interfacing - 9 × 70 cm [3½" × 27½"] (gusset)
8 Magnetic button - 2 cm [¾"] 1 pair
Thread to match fabric

8 Female   Male

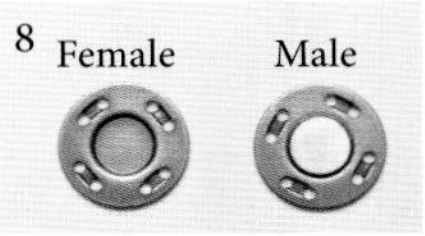

Doing the Appliqué

1. Tracing the Appliqué Pattern

Trace the appliqué design from the pattern onto tracing
paper using a dark marker. Use the beige check homespun
as the background fabric, cutting an 18 × 16 cm [7⅛" ×
6¼"] piece with a 0.7 cm [¼"] seam allowance. Copy the
design from the paper onto the fabric using a light table
with a marking pencil.
* If you do not have a light table, copy in daylight against
a transparent windowpane.

2. Preparing the Pieces

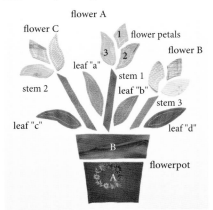

flower A
flower C
1 flower petals
3
flower B
2
leaf "a"
stem 1
stem 2
leaf "b"
stem 3
leaf "c"
leaf "d"
B
A
flowerpot

Cut 1.2 cm [½"] wide bias strips for stems 1 through 3; mark a sewing line 0.3 cm [⅛"] in from the edge of each strip. Trim each stem to the correct length after appliquéing. Draw around the templates on the wrong side of the fabric for pieces A and B of the flowerpot, adding a 0.7 cm [¼"] seam allowance. Using the templates, draw on the right side of the fabric for the flower and leaf pieces, adding a 0.3 to 0.5 cm [⅛"~¼"] seam allowance.

3. Appliquéing the Stems

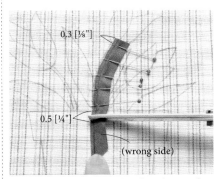

0.3 [⅛"]

0.5 [¼"]

(wrong side)

1 Appliqué "stem 1". With right sides together, lay the stem piece on the background piece, matching the sewing line to the marked stem line. Note that you will be folding the appliqué piece over, so pin the sewing line to the correct marked line. Pin in place; trim off the excess fabric.

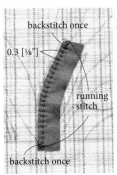

backstitch once

0.3 [⅛"]

running stitch

backstitch once

2 Take a backstitch at the start to secure, then use a running stitch to the end. Backstitch once more to secure the end.

(right side)

3 Fold the bias strip over right side out and finger press into place. Using a seam pressing tool, press down firmly to get a crisp seam.

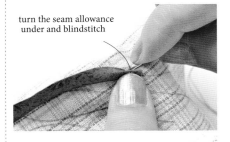

turn the seam allowance under and blindstitch

0.3 [⅛"]

4 Using the point of the needle, turn the seam allowance under so that the stem is the width that is marked on the background fabric. Begin to appliqué the side of the stem down using a blindstitch, turning the seam allowance under.

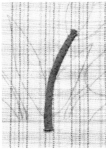

5 Continue to turn the seam allowance under the length of the stem as you blindstitch to the end. Knot off the end to finish.

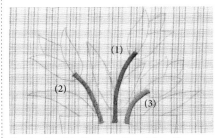

(1)

(2)

(3)

6 Appliqué both stems 2 and 3 in the same manner to complete the stems.

4. Appliquéing the Flowers

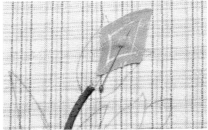

1 To appliqué flower A, with the wrong side down, lay petal 1 in place on the background fabric and pin in place.

Blindstitch

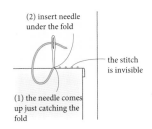

(2) insert needle under the fold

the stitch is invisible

(1) the needle comes up just catching the fold

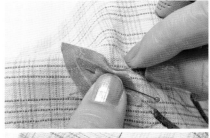

2 On the right side of the petal, turn the seam allowance under along the marked line using the point of the needle. Blindstitch along the marked line.

3 Trim any excess seam allowance along the left side of the petal.

4 Create crisp points by turning the seam allowance under in two steps, using the tip of the needle to push the seam allowance under.

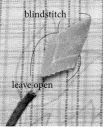

5 Blindstitch from the top point to the side point. As the bottom edges will be covered by petals 2 and 3, leave these open to keep the appliqué from getting too bulky.

6 Pin petal 2 in position with right side facing up. Turn the seam allowance on the right side of the petal under, taking one or two snips along the curve to help with ease. Begin to blindstitch from the bottom point along the right side toward the top point.

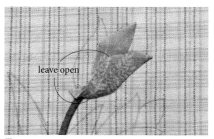

7 Create a crisp point and blindstitch along the top curve, covering petal 1 as shown. Leave the left side open where the edge will be covered by petal 3.

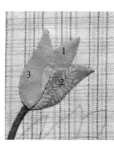

8 To complete flower A, pin petal 3 in place and begin to blindstitch from the bottom edge up the right side to the top point and back down the left side, turning the seam allowances under as you stitch.

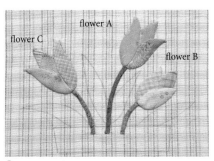

9 Appliqué flower B and C in the same way as you did for flower A.

5. Appliquéing the Leaves

1 Pin leaf A in place on the background fabric. Appliqué the leaf down turning the seam allowance under as you blindstitch. Snip into the seam allowance along the curves to help with ease. Create crisp points at both the top and bottom of the leaf.

2 Appliqué the remaining leaf B and leaf C in the same way as leaf A. When stitching leaf D, leave the bottom portion open where the flowerpot will cover it.

6. Appliquéing the Flowerpot

1 With the wrong side facing up, place the fabric for flowerpot A on the soft side of the non-slip board. Use the sharp edge of a Hera tool and press along the finished sewing line marks to create creases.

2 Following the creases just made, press the seam allowances in on either side of the flowerpot. Use the Hera pressing tool; press along the seam allowance for flat seams.

3 Pin the flowerpot in position on the background fabric. Blindstitch both of the sides, leaving the top and bottom open.

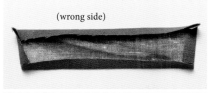

(wrong side)

blindstitch

4 Crease all four sides of the flower B appliqué piece using the same method as for flowerpot A. Pin in place, covering the open edges of the leaves, stems and flowerpot A. Blindstitch all four sides to finish the design.

Doing the Piecing

1. Making the Side Blocks and Sewing them to the Finished Appliqué Block

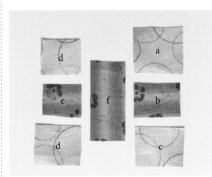

1 Referring to the pattern sheet insert, create the templates for pieces "a" through "f". Add a 0.7 cm [¼"] seam allowance when cutting out each piece. Draw the finished sewing lines on the wrong side of the fabric.

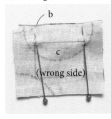

b

c

(wrong side)

2 Make the first segment on the right side of the block by pinning pieces "b" and "c", with right sides together, and matching the corner marks of the finished sewing lines.

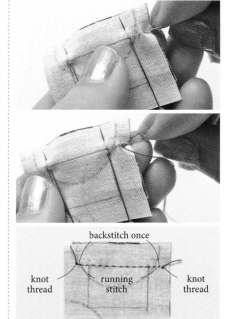

backstitch once

knot thread — running stitch — knot thread

3 Start 0.5 cm [¼"] outside of the corner mark and take 1 backstitch to secure. Sew across the finished sewing line using a running stitch, going 0.5 cm [¼"] outside of the opposite corner mark. Take another backstitch and knot off.

4 Trim any excess seam allowance down to 0.7 cm [¼"].

5 Fold the seam down toward piece "b". When hand-piecing seams, fold the finished seam to one side and press, leaving 0.1 cm [$^1/_{16}$"] showing over the fold. This helps to hide the seam when the piece is opened up. Place the pieced segment right side up on the soft side of the non-slip board. Use the Hera tool to press the seam flat.

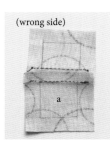
(wrong side)

a

6 To finish the segment on the right, sew piece "a" to piece "b". Fold the seam allowance down toward piece "b" (see steps 3-5 on the prior page).

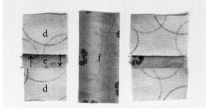
d

e

f

d

7 Make the segment on the left by sewing two "d" pieces on either side of piece "e". Fold the seam allowance down toward piece "e".

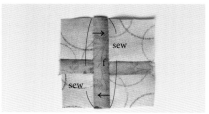
sew

f

sew

8 To make the first mini unit, sew the left and right segments to piece "f", folding the seam allowances toward piece "f". Repeat steps 1-8 to make a total of 8 of mini units.

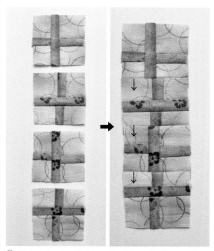

9 To make the right unit of the block, sew four of the mini units together vertically in whichever order is pleasing. Note that they will be off-center. Press the seam allowances toward the bottom.

10 Repeat step 9 for the remaining four mini units to make the left unit.

g

11 Using the template as a guide, cut two pieces for piece "g", adding a 0.7 cm [¼"] seam allowance. Sew each piece to the inner sides of the left and right units. Press the seam allowances toward piece "g" for both. This finishes units "A" and "B" for the side borders.

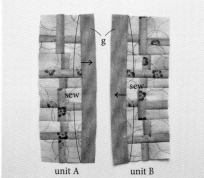
g

sew

sew

unit A   unit B

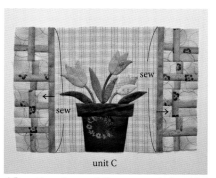
sew

sew

unit C

12 To make unit "C", sew units "A" and "B" to the appliquéd center block. Press the seam allowances toward the outside borders.

2. Making the Bottom Border

h

i

j

1 Using the template as a guide, cut one of each piece of "h", "i" and "j", adding a 0.7 cm [¼"] seam allowance.

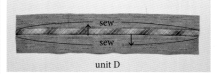
sew

sew

unit D

2 To make the bottom border, sew pieces "h" and "j" to center piece "i" from end to end. Press the seam allowances toward piece "i" to complete unit D.

C

sew

D

unit E

3 Sew unit C (the appliquéd unit) to unit D (the bottom border) from end to end. Press the seam allowance toward the bottom.

3. Making the Top Border

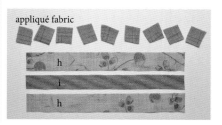
appliqué fabric

h

i

h

1 Using the template as a guide, cut two of piece "h" and one of piece "i", adding a 0.7 cm [¼"] seam allowance. Cut out the square appliqué pieces adding a seam allowance of 0.3 - 0.5 cm [⅛" - ¼"].

2 To make the top border, sew the "h" pieces to center piece "i" from end to end. Press the seam allowances toward piece "i".

(wrong side)

fold seam allowances

blindstitch

unit F

3 To finish the top border, use the sharp edge of a Hera tool and press along the finished sewing line marks to create creases for each square appliqué piece. Place the squares to be appliquéd in position as desired or as shown; pin in place, then blindstitch down to complete unit F.

sew

4 To complete the bag front top, sew unit F (the top border) to unit E. Press the seam allowance toward the top border.

Preparing the Top for Quilting

1. Marking the Quilting Lines on the Quilt Top

Lay the quilt top on the non-slip side of the non-slip board; using a marking pen/pencil of your choice, begin to draw the quilting lines (see diagram). You do not need to mark lines if you are planning to a) outline quilt around the appliqués b) quilt following the pattern on the fabric or c) stitch in the ditch (quilt along the seam lines).

2. Basting

quilt following the pattern on the fabric

1.5 [⅝"]
1.5 [⅝"]

quilt following the pattern on the fabric

quilting lines

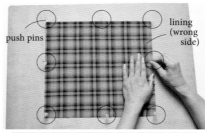

push pins

lining (wrong side)

batting

1 With the wrong side up, smooth the lining fabric out on a flat surface and pin or tape it to hold it taut. Begin by pinning or taping the four corners, followed by the center point of each side. With the batting cut to the same size as the lining fabric, lay it on top of the lining and re-pin or tape both layers to the flat surface.

2 Center the quilt top on top of the layers and pin down. Now you are ready to begin the basting process.

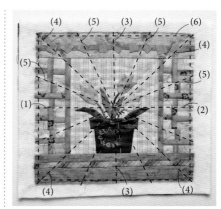

(4)　(5)　(3)　(5)　(6)

(4)

(5)

(5)

(1)　　　　　　　　　　(2)

(4)　　　(3)　　　(4)

3 Starting in the center of the quilt top with a length of knotted thread, baste all the way to the left edge. Use a spoon to help lift the needle from the surface as you baste. Knot the thread at the edge and cut it, leaving a 2-3 cm [¾" - 1¼"] tail. Repeat basting from the center out in a sunburst pattern following the order in the illustration above.

❧ Basting order
(1) from the center to the left edge, (2) from the center to the right edge, (3) vertically from the center, (4) diagonally, (5) between the diagonal and vertical lines, and (6) all around the outside of the block.

3. Quilting

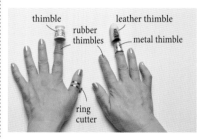

thimble · leather thimble
rubber thimbles · metal thimble
ring cutter

1 See the photo to the left for proper finger placement of quilting notions so as not to hurt your fingers while you quilt. There are many thimbles on the market, so find ones that are most comfortable for you when you work.

2 Using the non-slip board and weights, place the quilt as shown to keep it from moving while you quilt.

🌿 Quilting Thread Tip

Your finished quilting project will look best if you choose thread colors that are as close as possible to the fabrics on which you are working. If you do not have access to a wide variety of different colored thread, then it is often better to use thread that is darker in color than the fabric.

🌿 Quilting Order Tip

* Always start in the center of your quilt sandwich and work your way out toward the edges to keep the quilt as flat as possible.
(1) Begin by quilting the crosshatching on the background fabric of the appliquéd flowerpot.
(2) Quilt the flowerpot and the veins of the leaves. When quilting the flowerpot, follow the pattern of the print on the fabric.
(3) Outline quilt around the outside of the appliqués.
(4) Quilt inside all the borders as desired.
(5) Outline quilt around the square appliqué pieces.

3 When you have finished the quilting, carefully cut and pull the basting stitches out. Leave the basting around the outside edge of the block.

Quilting Step-by-Step

to finish, bring the needle out away from the stitches and cut the thread · buried knot · top · batting · backing

Beginning the Quilting Stitches

1 Knot the end of the thread and insert the needle into the quilt top and batting about 2 cm [¾"] away from where you will begin the first stitch. Bring the tip of the needle up and exit at the exact spot for the first stitch without going through the backing.

2 Pull the thread through until the knot is lying on the surface of the quilt top. Gently tug the thread to pop the knot through the quilt top to bury it in the batting. Take another stitch at the exact place where you started.

3 Insert the needle again at the first stitch perpendicular to the top and pull through the back, coming up very close to the first stitch. Insert the needle down again until you feel the tip of the needle with your finger under the quilt and immediately come back up.

Repeat this rocking motion until you have several stitches on your needle. Then use the thimble to push the needle through the quilt. Pull the thread to even the tension. Repeat until the end of your quilting line.

Ending the Quilting Stitches

1 Bring the needle up in the spot where you want the last stitch to be, leaving a space the width of two stitches in between .

2 Backstitch into the preceding space that was left open, bringing the needle up to create a final stitch.

3 Insert the needle in the last stitch again and work the needle through the batting, bringing the tip of the needle out about 2 cm [¾"] away from the last stitch. Carefully cut the thread close to the quilt top.

4. Quilting the Bag Back

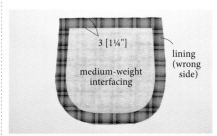

1 Fuse the medium-weight interfacing to the wrong side of the bag back lining. Place the bag back top on the lining with batting in between; baste.

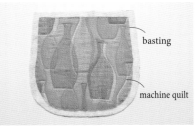

2 Machine quilt through all layers following the pattern on the fabric. Remove all basting stitches after quilting except for the basting stitches around the border.

5. Quilting the Gusset

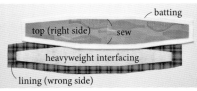

1 With right sides together, sew the two pieces of the gusset top along the bottom seam to create the gusset. Fuse the heavyweight interfacing to the wrong side of the lining; with wrong sides together, layer the lining and top with batting in between; baste.

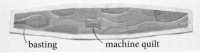

2 Machine quilt through all layers following the pattern on the fabric. Remove all basting stitches after quilting except for the basting stitches around the border.

Sewing the Bag Together

1. Sewing the Bag Body

1 Center the template on the lining side of the appliquéd bag front. Mark the finished sewing lines as well as all other marks on the template.

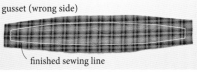

2 Using the respective templates, repeat the step above by copying all marks and finished sewing lines to the bag back and gusset pieces.

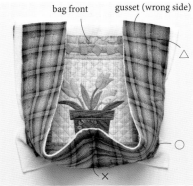

3 With right sides together, pin the gusset to the bag front matching the marks for the bag bottom center (✕), bag bottom sides (◯) and bag opening (△).

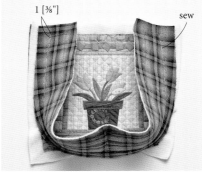

4 Baste along the finished sewing lines. Sew around the edges on the finished sewing lines starting and stopping up to 1 cm [⅜"] from the top of the bag opening.

5 Trim the seam allowances of all layers down to 0.7 cm [¼"] except for the gusset lining. Trim the gusset lining seam allowance down to 0.8 cm [⅜"].

6 Use an awl to help tuck the gusset seam allowance neatly around the raw edges to finish binding the seams. Pin in place.

blindstitch up to 1 [⅜"]
from the top opening

finished sewing line

bag front
lining

gusset lining

blindstitch

7 Starting at the bag opening on one side, begin to blindstitch the seam allowance 1 cm [⅜"] from the top edge; continue around to within 1 cm [⅜"] of the opposite side at the top.

bag front

bag back

8 To complete the bag body, repeat the directions and sew the bag back to the gusset. Bind the raw edges of the seam allowance.

9 Turn the bag body right side out and adjust the shape by pressing out the seam areas.

2. Making the Handles

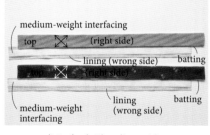

medium-weight interfacing

top   (right side)

lining (wrong side)   batting

(right side)

medium-weight
interfacing

lining
(wrong side)

batting

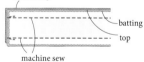

lining fused with medium-weight
interfacing

batting

top

machine sew

1 Fuse the interfacing to the wrong side of the handle lining. With right sides together, layer the top and lining with the batting on top; sew the seams.

2 Trim the batting close to the stitching. Repeat the above to make the second handle.

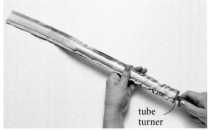

tube
turner

fold the end of the
fabric tube over

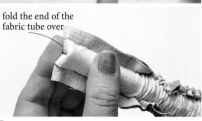

3 To make it easier, use a tube turner (see p. 53) to turn the fabric tube right side out. Insert the tube turner inside the fabric tube; fold the end of the fabric tube at the end.

hook

twist the end
of the hook
out of the
fabric tube

4 Slide the hook inside the tube turner; twist the hook clockwise as it comes out of the folded end to grab the fabric and hold it secure.

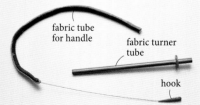

fabric tube
for handle

fabric turner
tube

hook

5 Pull the hook slowly and steadily back out of the tube turner to turn the fabric tube right side out as it passes through the tube.

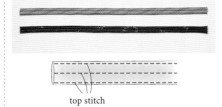

top stitch

6 Turn the second handle right side out using the same method with the tube turner. Adjust the shape, press and top stitch to finish.

3. Attaching the Handles, and Finishing the Opening

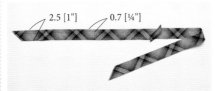

2.5 [1"]   0.7 [¼"]

1 Cut a piece of bias fabric 2.5 × 60 cm [1" × 23⅝"] to bind the bag opening using the plaid homespun (see p. 110 - p.111 for details on cutting bias binding).

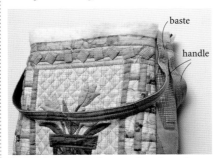

baste

handle

2 Mark the finished sewing line along the top at the bag opening. With right sides together, pin the handles on either side of the bag, centered on the gusset and aligning top edges; baste in place.

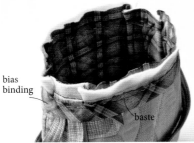

bias binding

baste

3 With right sides together and matching the finished sewing lines, pin the bias binding to the bag opening; baste. Sew the bias binding to the bag opening (see p. 110~111 for details on finishing the ends of the binding).

4 Trim the excess seam allowance of the bag body bag opening to match that of the bias binding.

5 Use the bias binding to fold over the raw seam allowances of the bag opening twice to the inside of the bag; pin in place. Blindstitch the binding down to the lining, being careful to stitch only through to the batting so that the stitches won't show on the outside.

4. Attaching the Magnetic Button

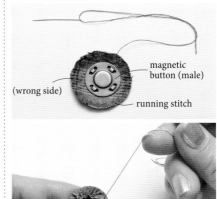

magnetic button (male)

(wrong side)

running stitch

1 Cut a circle of fabric that is at least 1 cm [⅜"] larger than the magnetic button out of the same fabric as the lining. Using a running stitch, sew around the edge of the fabric circle and place one side of the button in the center. Pull up the stitches to cover all except the center of the button; tie off. Repeat for the other side of the magnetic button.

bag opening bias binding

blindstitch

2 Place one covered button centered at the bag opening of the lining side with the top just touching the bias binding. Sew in place. Repeat on the other side with the other button.

Completed Bag

Before You Begin

Quilting Tips

❧ All measurements listed for the following projects are in centimeters (cm) and in inches [in brackets].

❧ The dimensions of the finished project (not including the handles) are listed for each, as well as shown in the drawings. Note that the quilted pieces tend to shrink somewhat, depending on the type of fabric used, the thickness of the batting, the amount of quilting and individual quilting technique.

❧ Typically, both the sewing and quilting thread should be the same color as the fabric you are working with. However, if you do not have a wide variety of thread colors or want a softer look that will still stand out, use a beige-colored thread.

❧ The words "top" and "outer" can be used interchangeably when talking about the front piece of fabric as opposed to the backing or lining.

❧ The icons denote the bias (✕) and the straight of grain (←→).

Bag Making Tips

⚜ Because the measurements of quilted pieces tend to shrink somewhat after quilting, you might need to adjust the final size of the templates when you construct each piece as this will allow for a better finished look.

Step 1: Make the bag front and bag back by first doing any called for appliqué and piecing, followed by layering the top, batting and lining together before quilting.

Step 2: Place the template on the lining side of the bag pieces and draw the finished sewing lines. If you need to resize the template, make sure it allows for a 0.7 cm [¼"] seam allowance all around.

Step 3: After drawing the finished sewing line on the bag pieces, adjust the gusset and any other pieces accordingly as necessary.

✻ The measurements shown in the dimensional diagrams are guides. Please measure your quilted bag pieces and adjust the measurements accordingly.

Basic Hand-Sewing Stitches and Methods

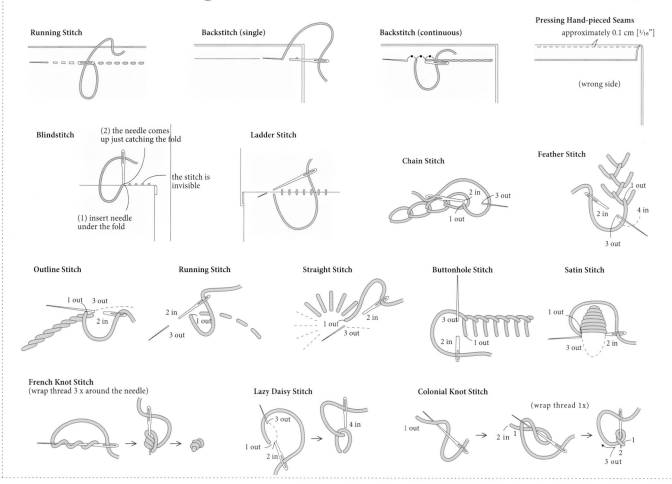

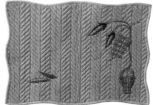

Strawberries   Peas

❧ Finished measurements
33.4 × 44.4 cm [13¼" × 17½"]

❧ Materials
[for either Strawberries or Peas (material for 1 placemat)]

Homespun - 33.5 × 44.5 cm [13¼" × 17½"] (top fabric)
Homespun - 36 × 47 cm [14⅛" × 18½"] (backing)
Assorted fat quarters or scraps - (appliqué)
Homespun - 3.5 × 160 cm [1⅜" × 63"] bias fabric (binding)
Batting - 36 × 47 cm [14⅛" × 18½"]

Strawberries
Embroidery floss - green, light green, mustard, brown, dk brown
Peas
Embroidery floss - olive

❧ Directions

1 Trace the appliqué design onto the placemat top of the design of your choice. Trace and cut out the appliqué pieces. Appliqué the pieces to the top. Embroider the designs according to the patterns.

2 With wrong sides together, layer the top and backing with the batting in between; baste and quilt. First quilt the background as shown in the dimensional diagrams. Then outline quilt around and inside the appliqués as shown or desired.

3 Make the bias binding. Bind the raw edges of the placemats around the outer edges. (see p. 110 - p. 111 for detailed instructions).

Dimensional Diagram

Strawberries
Placemat (1 of each)
top (homespun)
batting
backing (homespun)

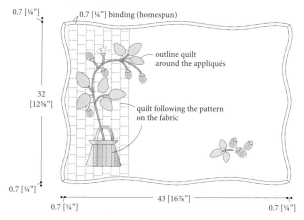

0.7 [¼"]
0.7 [¼"] binding (homespun)
outline quilt around the appliqués
quilt following the pattern on the fabric
32 [12⅝"]
0.7 [¼"]
0.7 [¼"]
43 [16⅞"]
0.7 [¼"]

＊ Use a narrow 1.2 - 1.5 cm [½" - ⅝"] wide bias binding for appliquéing the stems; add 0.3 - 0.5 cm [⅛" - ¼"] seam allowances for all appliqués other than the stems; add 0.7 cm [¼"] to the top fabric, and 2 cm [¾"] to the batting and backing.

Peas
Placemat (cut one of each)
Top (homespun)
(batting)
Backing (homespun)

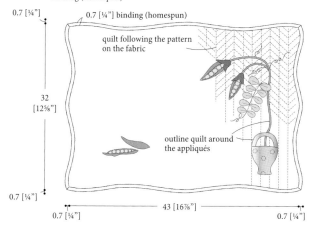

0.7 [¼"]
0.7 [¼"] binding (homespun)
quilt following the pattern on the fabric
32 [12⅝"]
outline quilt around the appliqués
0.7 [¼"]
0.7 [¼"]
43 [16⅞"]
0.7 [¼"]

＊ Use a narrow 1.2 - 1.5 cm [½" - ⅝"] wide bias fabric for appliquéing the stems; add 0.3 - 0.5 cm [⅛" - ¼"] seam allowances for all appliqués other than the stems; add 0.7 cm [¼"] to the top fabric, and 2 cm [¾"] to the batting and backing.

Earthenware Wall Quilt   * The full-size template/pattern can be found on Side A of the pattern sheet inserts.

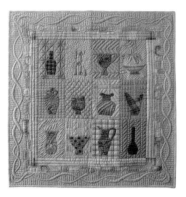

❧ Finished measurements
66.4 × 61.4 cm [26⅛" × 24⅛"]

❧ Materials
12 Assorted fat quarters or scraps - 16.5 × 11.5 cm [6½" × 4½"] each (block background "a")
Beige homespun - 35 × 70 cm [13¾" × 27½"] (borders a and b)
Plaid homespun - 71 × 66 cm [28" × 26"] (backing)
Assorted fat quarters or scraps (appliqué for inner border; pieces b, c, d)
Beige homespun - 3.5 × 265 cm [1⅜" × 104¼"] (binding)
Batting - 71 × 66 cm [28" × 26"]
White cotton thread (the thickness of medium-weight yarn) - enough for trapunto

❧ Directions
1 Trace the appliqué designs onto each of the background blocks. Trace and cut out the appliqué pieces referring to the pattern sheet inserts. Appliqué the pieces to the background pieces.
2 Referring to Diagrams 1 - 3 (to the right) sew the blocks together into rows to create the center.
3 Piece the inner border using the assorted scraps and fat quarters and sew it to the quilt center, followed by the outer border. Appliqué the shapes on top of the borders.
4 With wrong sides together, layer the top and backing with the batting in between; baste and quilt.
5 Make the binding and bind the quilt.
6 Follow the detailed instructions above to add trapunto to the cable design in the outer border area to finish the quilt.

Trapunto

❧ Materials
White yarn (med-weight, preferably cotton)
Trapunto needle

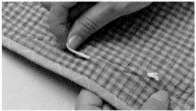

1 The cable design around the border is done using the trapunto quilting method. Double thread the trapunto needle. Take the finished quilt, and with the backing facing you, insert the needle between the backing and batting of the trapunto design area. Bring the needle back out when you have gone the length of the needle, pulling the yarn through almost all the way.

2 Insert the needle back in the same spot and continue feeding yarn along the cable design as in step 1. Continue to pull the yarn through evenly. When finished, adjust the yarn so that it lies flat. Cut the threads at the edge of the fabric.

3 If the trapunto area is wide, you may have to repeat this two or three times in the design area in order to achieve the desired amount of fill.

Sewing the Top Together

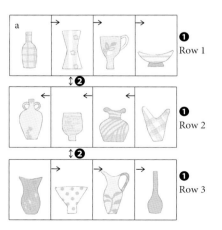

Diagram 1

Dimensional Diagram

Wall Quilt (1 of each)
quilt top (completed)
batting
backing (homespun)

* add 0.7 cm [¼"] seam allowance for piecing,
  0.3 - 0.5 cm [⅛" - ¼"] for the appliqué,
  and 3 cm [1¼"]for the batting and backing

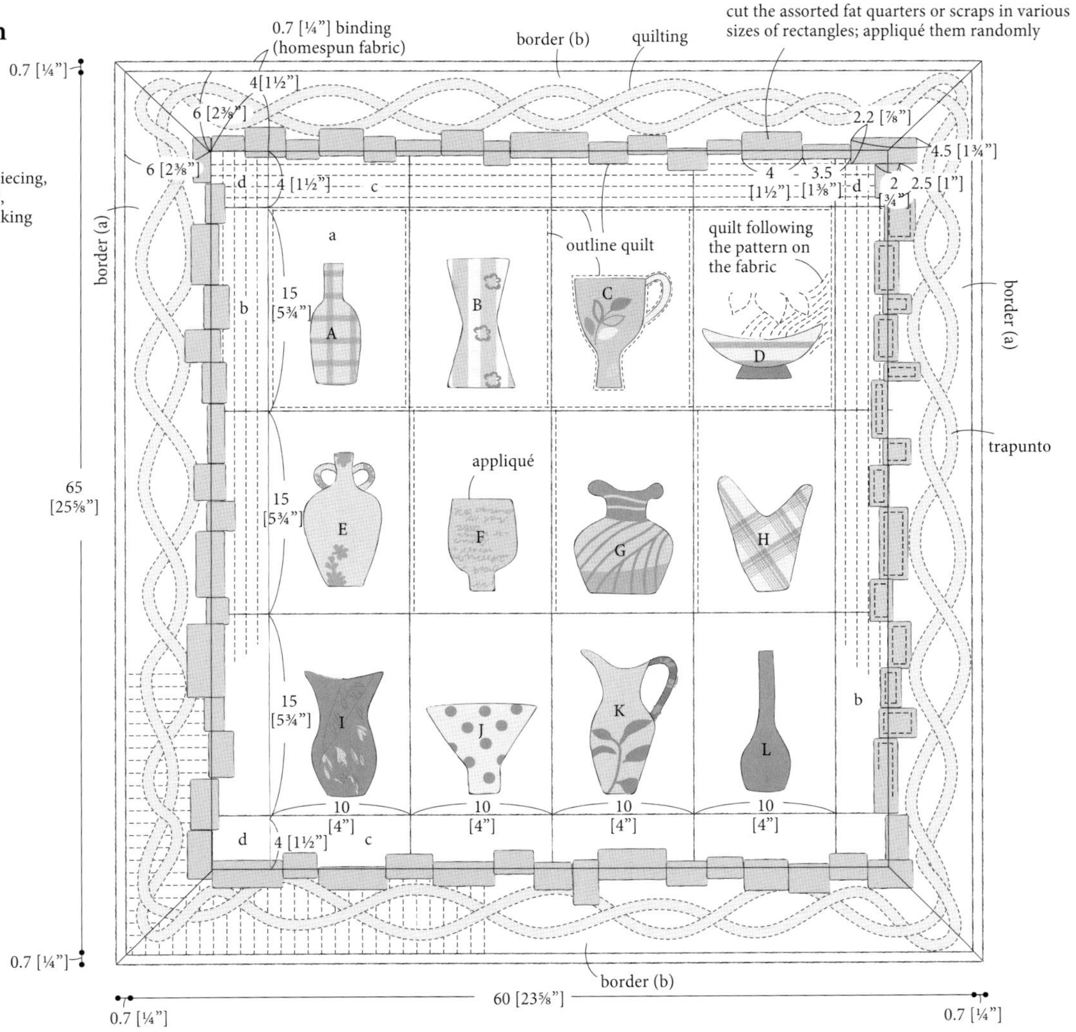

0.7 [¼"] binding
(homespun fabric)

border (b)   quilting   cut the assorted fat quarters or scraps in various
                          sizes of rectangles; appliqué them randomly

0.7 [¼"]

6 [2⅜"]
4 [1½"]
6 [2⅜"]

d   4 [1½"]   c

2.2 [⅞"]
4.5 [1¾"]
4   3.5
[1½"] [1⅜"] d   ¾"
2   2.5 [1"]

border (a)   border (a)

a

15 [5¾"]

b

A   B   C   D

outline quilt

quilt following
the pattern on
the fabric

trapunto

appliqué

15 [5¾"]

E   F   G   H

15 [5¾"]

I   J   K   L

b

65 [25⅝"]

10 [4"]   10 [4"]   10 [4"]   10 [4"]

d   4 [1½"]   c

0.7 [¼"]

border (b)

60 [23⅝"]

0.7 [¼"]   0.7 [¼"]

Diagram 2

d → c ← ← ← d

4

b   b

3   **3**

4

d → c ← ← ← d

Diagram 3

sew diagonally
from the mark
to the edge

6   border (b)   sew between marks   **6**

5

border (a)   sew diagonally
from the mark
to the edge

sew between marks   **5**   **5**   sew between marks

border (a)

5

6   border (b)   sew between marks   **6**

sew diagonally
from the mark
to the edge

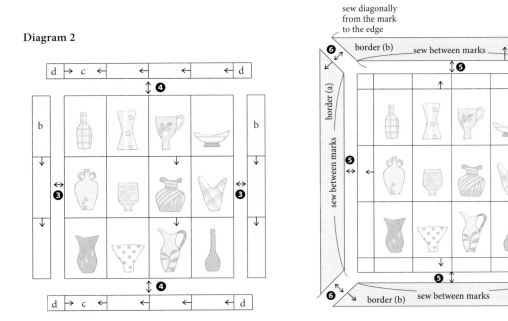

67

Floral Bouquet Wall Quilt ＊ The full-size template/pattern can be found on Side A of the pattern sheet inserts.

❧ Materials

Neutral print A - 44 × 41 cm [17" × 16⅛"] (appliqué background)

Print B - 90 × 60 cm [35⅜" × 23⅝"] (backing and 2.5 cm [1"] wide bias binding)

Taupe homespun - 30 × 55 cm [11¾" × 21⅝"] (border)

Assorted fat quarters or scraps - (appliqué)

Batting - 60 × 55 cm [23⅝" × 21⅝"]

Embroidery floss - lt beige, lt olive green, lt green, salmon pink

❧ Finished measurements
51 × 48 cm [20⅛" × 18⅞"]

❧ Directions

1 Referring to the pattern sheet inserts, appliqué and embroider the center background of the quilt. Appliqué the three dimensional flowers A through E while referring to Diagrams 1 through 5.

2 Cut out the borders and sew them together to create a frame. Place the border on top of the appliquéd background piece and center; baste around the edges to secure. Turn the seam allowance along the scalloped edge under with the point of the needle as you work and blindstitch to the background (Diagram 6). Cover and appliqué the designs on top of the blindstitched seams.

3 With wrong sides together, layer the top and backing with the batting in between; baste (be careful to not baste the three-dimensional flowers down) and quilt.

4 After quilting, remove the basting except for that around the edge. Bind the quilt using a 2.5 cm [1"] wide bias binding (Diagram 7).

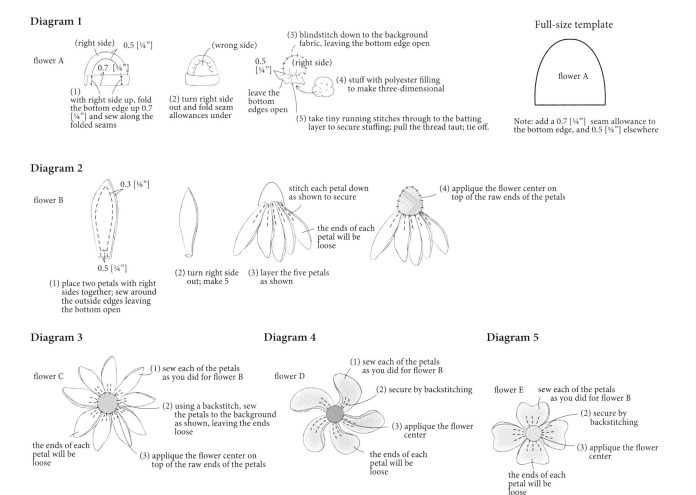

Diagram 1

flower A

(right side) 0.5 [¼"]
0.7 [¼"]

(1) with right side up, fold the bottom edge up 0.7 [¼"] and sew along the folded seams

(wrong side)

(2) turn right side out and fold seam allowances under

(3) blindstitch down to the background fabric, leaving the bottom edge open

0.5 [¼"]
(right side)

leave the bottom edges open

(4) stuff with polyester filling to make three-dimensional

(5) take tiny running stitches through to the batting layer to secure stuffing; pull the thread taut; tie off.

Full-size template

flower A

Note: add a 0.7 [¼"] seam allowance to the bottom edge, and 0.5 [¼"] elsewhere

Diagram 2

flower B

0.3 [⅛"]

0.5 [¼"]

(1) place two petals with right sides together; sew around the outside edges leaving the bottom open

(2) turn right side out; make 5

(3) layer the five petals as shown

stitch each petal down as shown to secure

the ends of each petal will be loose

(4) appliqué the flower center on top of the raw ends of the petals

Diagram 3

flower C

(1) sew each of the petals as you did for flower B

(2) using a backstitch, sew the petals to the background as shown, leaving the ends loose

the ends of each petal will be loose

(3) appliqué the flower center on top of the raw ends of the petals

Diagram 4

flower D

(1) sew each of the petals as you did for flower B

(2) secure by backstitching

(3) appliqué the flower center

the ends of each petal will be loose

Diagram 5

flower E

sew each of the petals as you did for flower B

(2) secure by backstitching

(3) appliqué the flower center

the ends of each petal will be loose

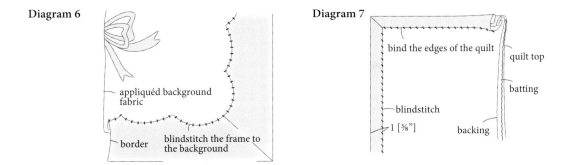

Diagram 6

appliquéd background fabric

border   blindstitch the frame to the background

Diagram 7

bind the edges of the quilt

quilt top

batting

blindstitch

1 [⅜"]

backing

Dimensional Diagram

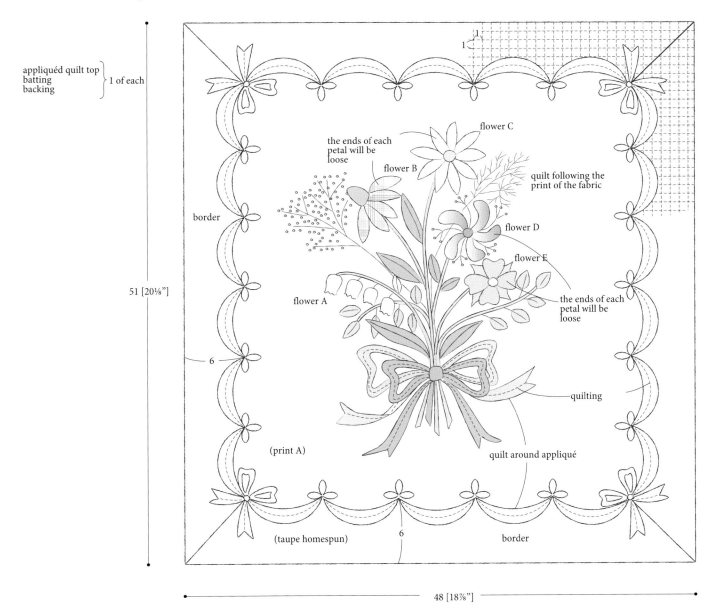

appliquéd quilt top
batting
backing   } 1 of each

border

51 [20⅛"]

6

(print A)

(taupe homespun)   6   border

the ends of each petal will be loose

flower B

flower C

flower A

flower D

flower E

the ends of each petal will be loose

quilt following the print of the fabric

quilting

quilt around appliqué

1
1

48 [18⅞"]

* Use 1.2 - 1.5 cm [½" - ⅝"]wide bias binding to applique the stems; add 0.3 - 0.5 cm [⅛" - ¼"] seam allowance for all appliqués, add 1 cm [⅜"] for the appliqué background, 0.7 cm [¼"] for the border, and add 3 cm [1¼"] to the batting and backing.

❧ Materials

Print - 20 × 30 cm [7⅞" × 11¾"] (top)
Brown homespun - 10 × 10 cm [4" × 4"] (bottom)
Muslin - 23 × 45 cm [9" × 17¾"] (facing - body, bottom)
Polka-dot print - 25 × 25 cm [9¾" × 9¾"] (handle top)
Beige homespun - 4 × 32 cm [1½" × 12⅝"] (handle backing)
Assorted fat quarters or scraps (appliqué)
Vinyl-coated print - 20 × 40 cm [7⅞" × 15¾"] (lining - body, bottom)
Batting - 23 × 45 cm [9" × 17¾"]
Lightweight interfacing - 2 × 30 cm [¾" × 11¾"](handle)
Embroidery floss - lt beige, brown, dk brown, green, pale green, dk green, beige, pink, med. pink, dk pink, black, grey

❧ Finished measurements
18.5 × 8.6 cm [7¼" × 3⅜"]

❧ Directions

1 Trace the appliqué design onto the water bottle holder top fabric. Trace and cut out the appliqué pieces. Appliqué the pieces to the top. Layer the top and facing with wrong sides together and batting in between; baste, then quilt.

2 Layer the top and facing for the water bottle holder bottom with wrong sides together and batting in between; baste, then quilt.

3 With right sides together, sew the body and bottom together; trim the excess seam allowance of the batting and facing even with the top.

4 Cut out the lining; fold with right sides together and sew along the seam, leaving an opening for turning right side out. Cut out the bottom from the lining print. With right sides together, sew the bottom to the lining.

5 With right sides together, sew the outer appliquéd piece to the lining around the water bottle holder opening (Diagram 1). Turn it right side out through the opening in the lining; blindstitch closed.

6 Push the lining to the inside of the water bottle holder; adjust the shape; top stitch along the opening edge (Diagram 2).

7 Make the handle (Diagram 3) and sew it to the holder (Diagram 2) to finish.

Dimensional Diagram

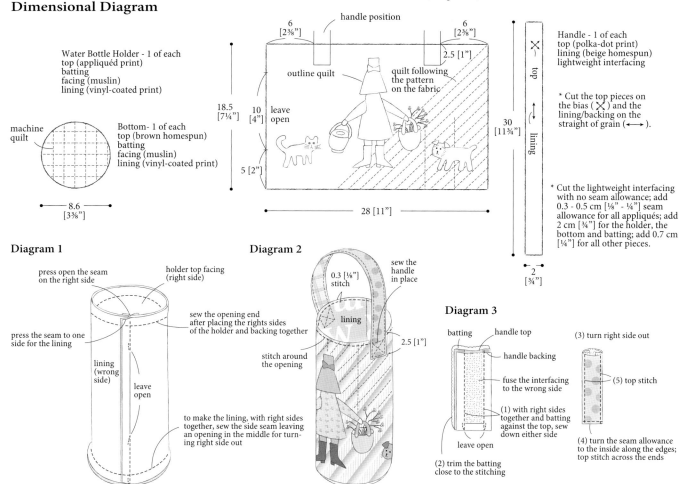

* The full-size template/pattern can be found on Side B of the pattern sheet inserts.

❧ Materials

Lt brown plaid homespun - 23 × 13 cm [9" × 5⅛"] (case body front)

Grey homespun - 23 × 13 cm [9" × 5⅛"] (case body back)

Brown homespun - 30 × 40 cm [11¾" × 15¾"] (case and gusset lining, zipper opening facing)

Check homespun - 30 × 30 cm [11¾" × 11¾"] (gusset)

Print - 17 × 22 cm [6" × 8⅝"] 2 each (pockets)

Plaid homespun - 25 × 25 cm [9¾" × 9¾"] (handle)

Assorted fat quarters or scraps - (appliqué)

Batting - 25 × 37 cm [9¾" × 14½"]

Lightweight interfacing - 22 × 11 cm [8⅝" × 4⅜"](case body lining)

Med-weight interfacing - 36 × 4 cm [14⅛" × 1½"] (gusset lining and handle backing)

1 Zipper (polka-dot zipper tape) - 17 cm [6"]

Embroidery floss - grey, black, dk brown

❧ Directions

Follow the detailed diagrams below to complete the project.

❧ Finished measurements

21.5 × 11 cm [8½" × 4⅜"]

2 cm [¾"] (gusset width)

* Do not add seam allowance to the interfacing for the case body lining, gusset lining or handle backing. Use a narrow 1.2 - 1.5 cm [½" - ⅝"] wide bias binding for appliquéing the stem; add 0.3 - 0.5 cm [⅛" - ¼"] seam allowances for all appliqués other than the stems; add 0.5 cm [¼"] to the zipper opening facing, and 0.7 cm [¼"] for all else.

Dimensional Diagram

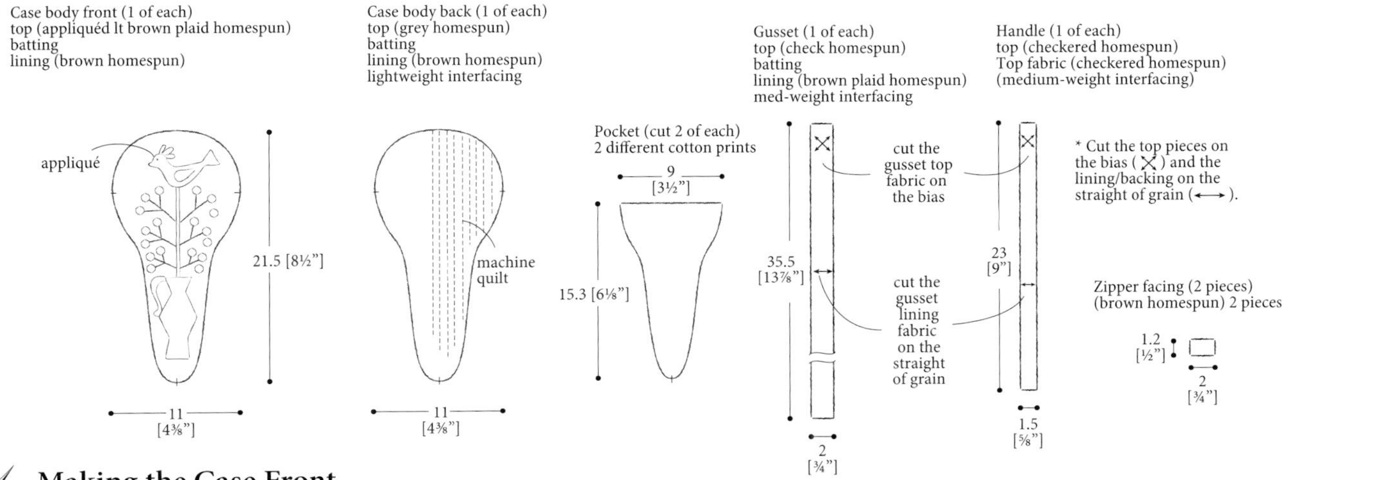

Case body front (1 of each)
top (appliquéd lt brown plaid homespun)
batting
lining (brown homespun)

Case body back (1 of each)
top (grey homespun)
batting
lining (brown homespun)
lightweight interfacing

Gusset (1 of each)
top (check homespun)
batting
lining (brown plaid homespun)
med-weight interfacing

Handle (1 of each)
top (checkered homespun)
Top fabric (checkered homespun)
(medium-weight interfacing)

appliqué

21.5 [8½"]

11 [4⅜"]

machine quilt

11 [4⅜"]

Pocket (cut 2 of each)
2 different cotton prints

9 [3½"]

15.3 [6⅛"]

cut the gusset top fabric on the bias

35.5 [13⅞"]

cut the gusset lining fabric on the straight of grain

2 [¾"]

* Cut the top pieces on the bias (✕) and the lining/backing on the straight of grain (⟷).

23 [9"]

1.5 [⅝"]

Zipper facing (2 pieces)
(brown homespun) 2 pieces

1.2 [½"]

2 [¾"]

1. **Making the Case Front**

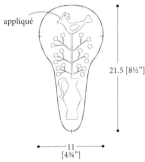

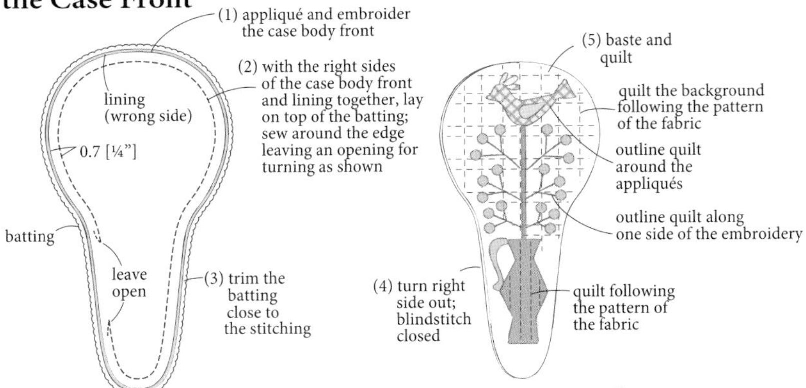

(1) appliqué and embroider the case body front

(2) with the right sides of the case body front and lining together, lay on top of the batting; sew around the edge leaving an opening for turning as shown

lining (wrong side)

0.7 [¼"]

batting

leave open

(3) trim the batting close to the stitching

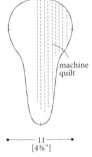

(5) baste and quilt

quilt the background following the pattern of the fabric

outline quilt around the appliqués

outline quilt along one side of the embroidery

(4) turn right side out; blindstitch closed

quilt following the pattern of the fabric

2. **Making the Case Back**

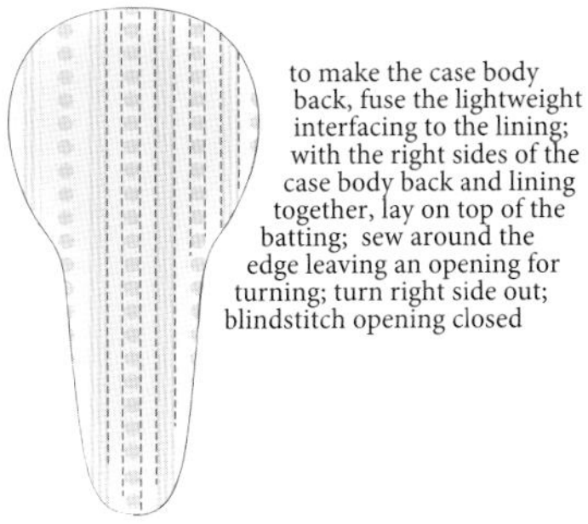

to make the case body back, fuse the lightweight interfacing to the lining; with the right sides of the case body back and lining together, lay on top of the batting; sew around the edge leaving an opening for turning; turn right side out; blindstitch opening closed

3. **Adding the Pockets**

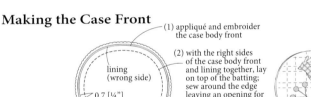

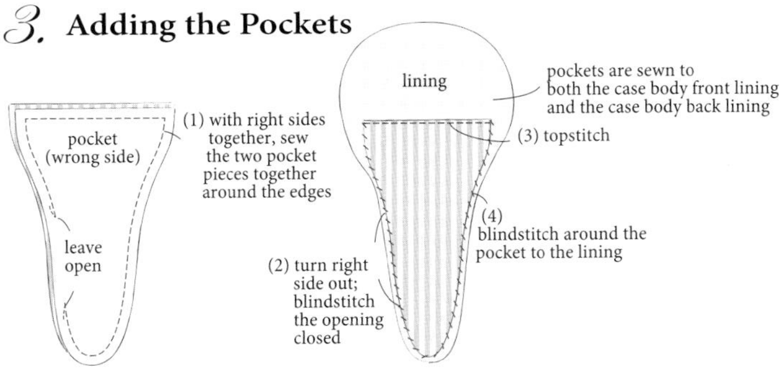

pocket (wrong side)

leave open

(1) with right sides together, sew the two pocket pieces together around the edges

lining

pockets are sewn to both the case body front lining and the case body back lining

(3) topstitch

(4) blindstitch around the pocket to the lining

(2) turn right side out; blindstitch the opening closed

4. **Making the Gusset**

top   batting   med-weight interfacing

leave open

gusset lining (wrong side)

0.7 [¼"]

(1) fuse the med-weight interfacing to the wrong side of the gusset lining; with the right sides of the gusset top and gusset lining together, lay on top of the batting; sew around the edges, leaving one end open to turn right side out

(2) turn right side out; blindstitch closed

(3) machine quilt

5. Complete the Case

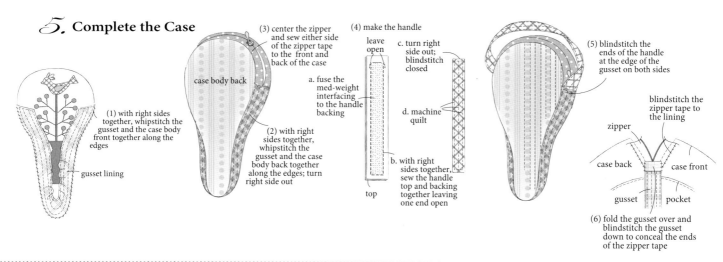

(1) with right sides together, whipstitch the gusset and the case body front together along the edges

gusset lining

(3) center the zipper and sew either side of the zipper tape to the front and back of the case

case body back

(2) with right sides together, whipstitch the gusset and the case body back together along the edges; turn right side out

(4) make the handle

leave open

c. turn right side out; blindstitch closed

a. fuse the med-weight interfacing to the handle backing

d. machine quilt

b. with right sides together, sew the handle top and backing together leaving one end open

top

(5) blindstitch the ends of the handle at the edge of the gusset on both sides

blindstitch the zipper tape to the lining

zipper

case back   case front

gusset   pocket

(6) fold the gusset over and blindstitch the gusset down to conceal the ends of the zipper tape

---

Shown on p. *17* ❧ Mini Card Holders

✻ The full-size template/pattern can be found on Side B of the pattern sheet inserts.

 A

 B

❧ Finished measurements
Mini Card Holder A - 8 × 12.5 cm [3⅛" × 5"]
Mini Card Holder B - 10.5 × 11 cm [4⅛" × 4⅜"]

❧ Materials

Mini Card Holder A
Grey print - 10 × 30 cm [4" × 11¾"] (pieces a, b)
Plaid homespun - 10 × 30 cm [4" × 11¾"] (lining)
Brown print - 20 × 20 cm [7⅞" × 7⅞"] (handle)
Assorted fat quarters or scraps - (piece c, appliqué)
Batting - 20 × 20 cm [7⅞" × 7⅞"]
Interfacing - 17 × 1.5 cm [6" × ⅝"] (handle)
Embroidery floss - green, dk brown
Candlewicking thread - lt beige
1 Button - 1.3 cm [½"] diameter
1 Snap
Hook-and-loop tape - 2 × 5 cm [¾" × 2"]

Mini Card Holder B
Brown print fabric - 10 × 25 cm [4" × 9¾"] (piece b)
Plaid homespun - 12 × 25 cm [4¾" × 9¾"] (lining)
Assorted fat quarters or scraps - (pieces, handle, braid, and appliqué)
Batting - 12 × 25 cm [4¾" × 9¾"]
1 Button - 1 cm [⅜"] diameter
1 Snap
Hook-and-loop tape - 2 × 5 cm [¾" × 2"]

❧ Directions
Refer to the diagrams and follow the directions for Mini Card Holder A and B .

Mini Card Holder "A"

Dimensional Diagram

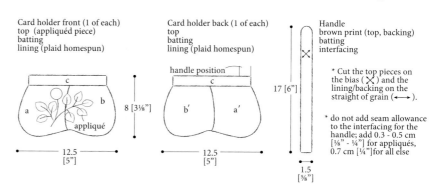

Card holder front (1 of each)
top (appliquéd piece)
batting
lining (plaid homespun)

Card holder back (1 of each)
top
batting
lining (plaid homespun)

handle position

appliqué

8 [3⅛"]

12.5 [5"]

b'   a'

12.5 [5"]

Handle
brown print (top, backing)
batting
interfacing

17 [6"]

1.5 [⅝"]

✻ Cut the top pieces on the bias (✕) and the lining/backing on the straight of grain (⟷).

✻ do not add seam allowance to the interfacing for the handle; add 0.3 - 0.5 cm [⅛" - ¼"] for appliqués, 0.7 cm [¼"]for all else

1. Making the Handle

leave open

batting

top

turn right side out

(2) sew

(1) fuse the interfacing to the wrong side of the handle backing

(3) trim the batting close to the stitching

(4) topstitch

2. Making the Card Holder Body

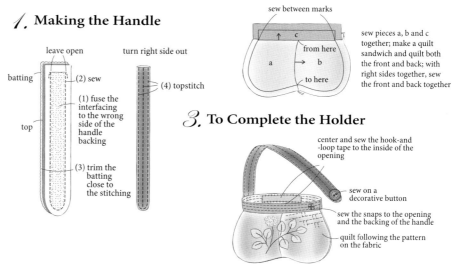

sew between marks

c

from here

to here

a

b

sew pieces a, b and c together; make a quilt sandwich and quilt both the front and back; with right sides together, sew the front and back together

3. To Complete the Holder

center and sew the hook-and-loop tape to the inside of the opening

sew on a decorative button

sew the snaps to the opening and the backing of the handle

quilt following the pattern on the fabric

Mini Card Holder "B"

Dimensional Diagram

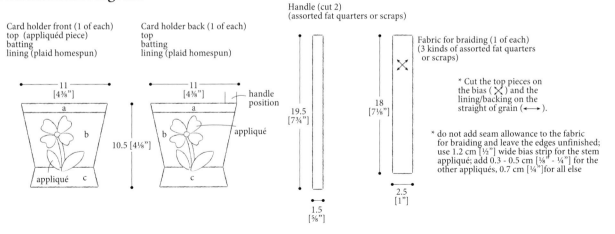

Card holder front (1 of each)
top (appliquéd piece)
batting
lining (plaid homespun)

Card holder back (1 of each)
top
batting
lining (plaid homespun)

Handle (cut 2)
(assorted fat quarters or scraps)

Fabric for braiding (1 of each)
(3 kinds of assorted fat quarters
or scraps)

11
[4⅜"]

11
[4⅜"]

handle
position

appliqué

a

b

appliqué   c

a

b

c

appliqué

10.5 [4⅛"]

19.5
[7¾"]

18
[7⅛"]

1.5
[⅝"]

2.5
[1"]

* Cut the top pieces on
the bias (✕) and the
lining/backing on the
straight of grain (←→).

* do not add seam allowance to the fabric
for braiding and leave the edges unfinished;
use 1.2 cm [½"] wide bias strip for the stem
appliqué; add 0.3 - 0.5 cm [⅛" - ¼"] for the
other appliqués, 0.7 cm [¼"] for all else

1. Making the Handle

2. Making the Card Holder Body

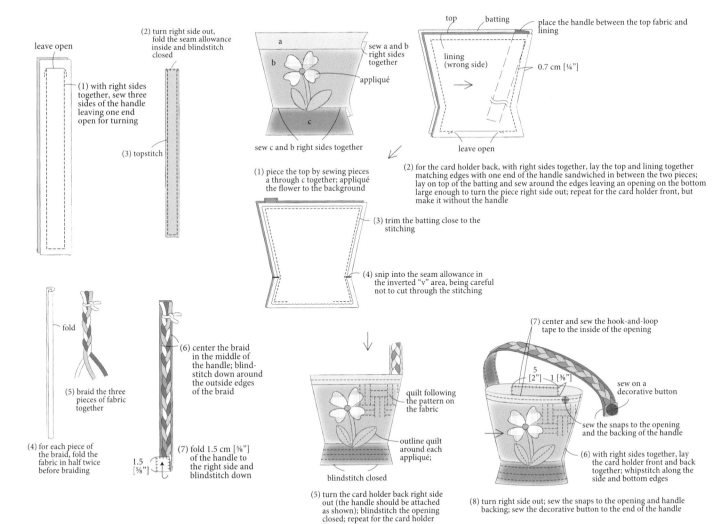

leave open

(1) with right sides
together, sew three
sides of the handle
leaving one end
open for turning

(2) turn right side out,
fold the seam allowance
inside and blindstitch
closed

(3) topstitch

fold

(4) for each piece of
the braid, fold the
fabric in half twice
before braiding

(5) braid the three
pieces of fabric
together

(6) center the braid
in the middle of
the handle; blind-
stitch down around
the outside edges
of the braid

(7) fold 1.5 cm [⅝"]
of the handle to
the right side and
blindstitch down

1.5
[⅝"]

a

b

appliqué

c

sew a and b
right sides
together

sew c and b right sides together

(1) piece the top by sewing pieces
a through c together; appliqué
the flower to the background

(3) trim the batting close to the
stitching

(4) snip into the seam allowance in
the inverted "v" area, being careful
not to cut through the stitching

top   batting

place the handle between the top fabric and
lining

lining
(wrong side)

0.7 cm [¼"]

leave open

(2) for the card holder back, with right sides together, lay the top and lining together
matching edges with one end of the handle sandwiched in between the two pieces;
lay on top of the batting and sew around the edges leaving an opening on the bottom
large enough to turn the piece right side out; repeat for the card holder front, but
make it without the handle

quilt following
the pattern on
the fabric

outline quilt
around each
appliqué;

blindstitch closed

(5) turn the card holder back right side
out (the handle should be attached
as shown); blindstitch the opening
closed; repeat for the card holder
front

(7) center and sew the hook-and-loop
tape to the inside of the opening

5
[2"]   1 [⅜"]

sew on a
decorative button

sew the snaps to the opening
and the backing of the handle

(6) with right sides together, lay
the card holder front and back
together; whipstitch along the
side and bottom edges

(8) turn right side out; sew the snaps to the opening and handle
backing; sew the decorative button to the end of the handle

Shown on p. *16* 🌀 **Rose Pouch**

* The full-size template/pattern can be found on Side B of the pattern sheet inserts.

Dimensional Diagram

* Add 0.5 cm [¼"] for the zipper tab, petal A, petal B, leaves, and flannel; 0.7 cm [¼"] for the pouch body front and back and batting; and 2 cm [¾"] for the lining

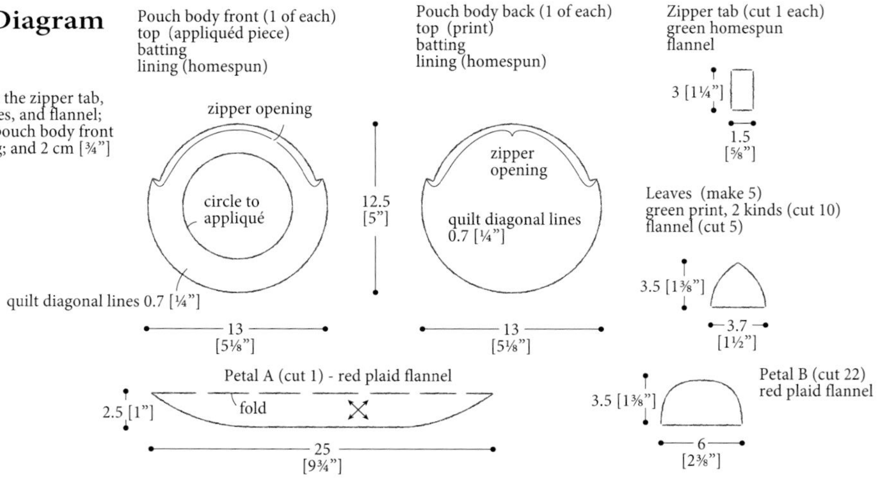

Pouch body front (1 of each)
top (appliquéd piece)
batting
lining (homespun)

zipper opening

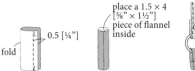
circle to appliqué

12.5 [5"]

quilt diagonal lines 0.7 [¼"]

13 [5⅛"]

Pouch body back (1 of each)
top (print)
batting
lining (homespun)

zipper opening

quilt diagonal lines 0.7 [¼"]

13 [5⅛"]

Zipper tab (cut 1 each)
green homespun
flannel

3 [1¼"]

1.5 [⅝"]

Leaves (make 5)
green print, 2 kinds (cut 10)
flannel (cut 5)

3.5 [1⅜"]

3.7 [1½"]

Petal A (cut 1) - red plaid flannel

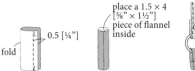
2.5 [1"] — fold — ✕

25 [9¾"]

Petal B (cut 22)
red plaid flannel

3.5 [1⅜"]

6 [2⅜"]

* Cut the top pieces on the bias (✕) and the lining/backing on the straight of grain (↔).

Finished measurements
13 cm [5⅛"] in diameter

Materials

Print fabric - 15 × 30 cm [5⅞" × 11¾"] (pouch body front, pouch body back)
Homespun - 35 × 35 cm [13¾" × 13¾"] (pouch body lining, and 2.5 × 40 cm [1"× 15¾"] wide bias fabric)
Green print - two kinds (leaves)
Green homespun - a scrap (zipper tab)
Homespun - 10 × 10 cm [4" × 4"] (appliqué background circle fabric)
Red plaid flannel - 30 × 45 cm [11¾" × 17¾"] (petals A and B)
Batting - 17 × 35 cm [6" × 13¾"]
Flannel - 5 × 26 cm [2" × 10¼"] (used as thin batting)
1 Zipper - 15.5 cm [6⅛"] in length
Jump ring - (end of strap/zipper tab)
1 Handle strap

Directions

1 Appliqué the background circle fabric to the center of the pouch body front. With right sides together, place the pouch body front and lining together on top of the batting; sew the zipper opening area along the sewing line by machine.

2 Turn right side out; baste, then quilt. Quilt straight lines on the diagonal across the entire piece in 0.7 cm [¼"] intervals.

3 Make the pouch body back following the same directions as above without the added appliquéd circle fabric.

4 With right sides together, sew the pouch body front and pouch body back together, except for the zipper opening area that is already finished. With right sides together, sew the zipper to the finished zipper opening; blindstitch the zipper tape to the lining. Use the 2.5 cm [1"] bias fabric to bind the raw edges.

5 Make the zipper tab (Diagram 1); fold in half through the jump ring. With right sides together, sew the zipper tab to the left side of the zipper opening, centered on the center seam (Diagram 5).

6 Make the three-dimensional petals and leaves referring to Diagrams 2 through 4.

7 Sew the leaves as you desire around the appliquéd circle on the pouch body front as shown in Diagram 5. Sew the petals (B) to the background on top of the leaves, evenly distributing them in a circular fashion starting from the bottom layer. Leave the very center open to sew on petal A to finish the flower. Attach the strap to finish the pouch.

Diagram 1

fold — 0.5 [¼"] — fold

place a 1.5 × 4 [⅝" × 1½"] piece of flannel inside

strap
jump ring
baste

(1) fold right sides together lengthwise; sew the side seam

(2) turn right side out; center the seam; press

(3) fold in half through the jump ring; baste

Diagram 2

fold — leave open 5 [2"] — petal A (wrong side)

0.5 [¼"]

(1) fold with right sides together; sew along the open edge, leaving the center open for turning

fold

(2) turn it right side out; blindstitch the opening closed; roll up to make the center of the flower

Diagram 3

petal B (wrong side)

(right side)

(3) sew a running stitch; pull up stitches; tie off

(1) with right sides together, sew two sides of petal B together around the edges leaving the bottom open; make 11 petals

(2) turn right side out, fold the raw edges to the inside; blindstitch closed; sew a running stitch along the lower edge; pull up stitches

Diagram 4

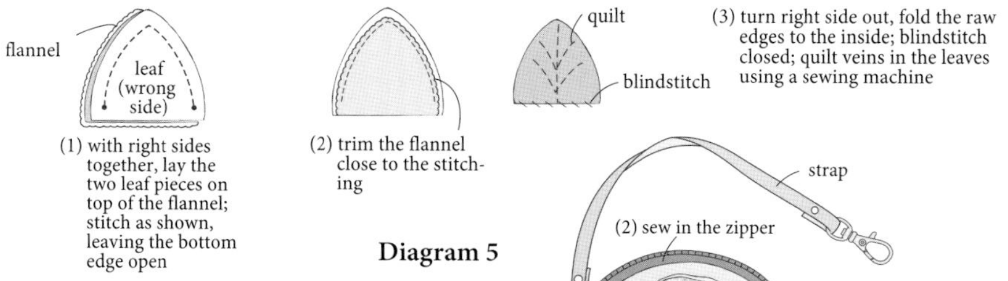

flannel

leaf (wrong side)

quilt
blindstitch

(3) turn right side out, fold the raw edges to the inside; blindstitch closed; quilt veins in the leaves using a sewing machine

(1) with right sides together, lay the two leaf pieces on top of the flannel; stitch as shown, leaving the bottom edge open

(2) trim the flannel close to the stitching

Diagram 5

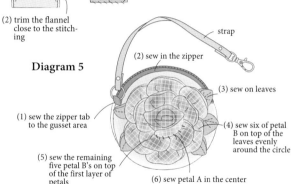

strap

(2) sew in the zipper

(3) sew on leaves

(4) sew six of petal B on top of the leaves evenly around the circle

(1) sew the zipper tab to the gusset area

(5) sew the remaining five petal B's on top of the first layer of petals

(6) sew petal A in the center

Shown on p. *16* 🌀 **Wheelbarrow Pouch**

✳ The full-size template/pattern can be found on Side B of the pattern sheet inserts.

🌿 **Materials**

Print - 11 × 18 cm [4⅜" × 7⅛"] (pouch body back)
Homespun - 25 × 40 cm [9¾" × 15¾"] (lining)
Homespun - 8 × 30 cm [3⅛" × 11¾"] (pieces e, d)
Homespun - 20 × 20 cm [7⅞" × 7⅞"] (handle, piece f, zipper tab)
Assorted fat quarters or scraps - (appliqué, pieces a, b, c)
Homespun - 3.5 × 50 cm [1⅜" × 19¾"] (bias binding)
Batting - 25 × 40 cm [9¾" × 15¾"]
Lightweight interfacing - 6 × 26 cm [2⅜" × 10¼"] (gusset)
Medium-weight interfacing - 1.5 × 15 cm [⅝" × 5⅞"] (handle)
1 Zipper - 19 cm [7½"]
2 Flower-shaped buttons - 1.5 cm [⅝"]
Jump ring - (zipper pull)
Embroidery floss - mustard, wine, green, dk grey

🌿 **Finished measurements**
9.5 × 22 cm [3¾" × 8⅝"]
6 cm [2⅜"] (gusset width)

🌿 **Directions**

1 Piece the pouch body front; appliqué and embroider the designs on the top. With wrong sides together, layer the pouch body front and lining with batting in between; baste; quilt.

2 With wrong sides together, layer the pouch body back and lining with batting in between; baste; quilt.

3 Piece the gusset top; fuse the lightweight interfacing to the wrong side of the gusset lining. With wrong sides together, layer the gusset top and lining with batting in between; baste; quilt by machine.

4 Make the handle by referring to the directions for the drawstring bag (p. 91). Baste the handle in place on the side of the gusset (Diagram 1).

5 With right sides together, sew the pouch body front and pouch body back to the gusset; trim the seam allowance down to 0.7 cm [¼"] except for the gusset lining; use the gusset lining to bind the raw edges; blindstitch down.

6 Use the bias binding to bind the zipper opening; sew the zipper to the top of the inside of the zipper opening using a backstitch (Diagram 3).

7 Make the zipper tab (Diagram 2).

8 Fold the zipper tab through a jump ring, then attach to the zipper clasp; sew the two buttons back to back on the end of the zipper tab (Diagram 3).

Dimensional Diagram

Pouch body front (1 of each)
top (appliquéd piece)
batting
lining (homespun)

appliqué
a
b   b
c
outline quilt around each appliqué
quilt

8.8 [3⅞"]

16 [6¼"]

Pouch body back (1 of each)
top (print)
batting
lining (homespun)

quilt
1.5 [⅝"]
1.5 [⅝"]

16 [6¼"]

Handle
top and backing (homespun)
batting
medium-weight interfacing

15 [5⅞"]
top (cut on the bias)
backing (cut on the straight grain)
1.5 [⅝"]

6.5 [2⅜"]
Zipper tab (cut 1)
homespun
do not add seam allowance
3 [1¼"]

* Cut the top pieces on the bias (✕) and the lining/backing on the straight of grain (⟷).

6 [2⅜"]
d f   e   f d
each 1.5 [⅝"]   each 1.5 [⅝"]
20 [7⅞"]
26 [10¼"]

Gusset (1 of each)
top (piecing)
batting
lining (homespun)
lightweight interfacing
quilt as desired

* Do not add any seam allowance to the interfacing pieces; add 2 cm [¾"] to the batting and pouch body and gusset linings; add 0.3 - 0.5 cm [⅛" - ¼"] to the appliqués; and 0.7 cm [¼"] for all else.

Diagram 1

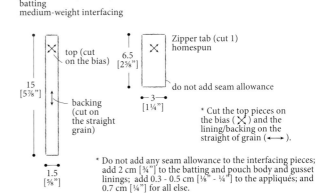

lining (fuse lightweight interfacing to the wrong side)
batting
top
1.5 [⅝"]
gusset (right side)
(2) baste
(1) piece the gusset; press the seams toward the darker fabric
(4) baste the handle in place
(3) machine quilt

Diagram 2

(1) 0.5 [¼"]
fold
zipper tab (wrong side)
0.5 [¼"]
(3) sew
(2) press the seam allowance open and center
(5) topstitch
(4) turn right side out, fold the seam allowance under 0.5 [¼"]; blindstitch closed

Diagram 3

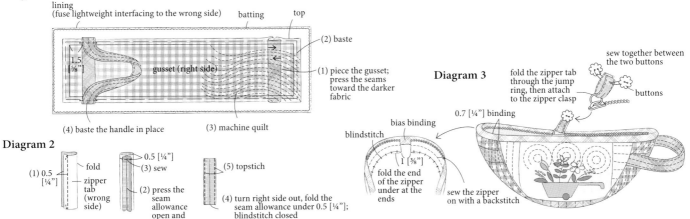

sew together between the two buttons
fold the zipper tab through the jump ring, then attach to the zipper clasp
buttons
0.7 [¼"] binding
bias binding
blindstitch
1 [⅜"]
fold the end of the zipper under at the ends
sew the zipper on with a backstitch

75

❧ Finished measurements
22 × 16 cm [8⅝" × 6¼"]
when folded in half (A5 size)

❧ Materials
Beige striped linen - 22 × 70 cm [8⅝" × 27½"] (cover, inner facings A, B)
Plaid homespun - 7 × 35 cm [2¾" × 13¾"] (bottom section of cover)
Polka-dot print - 25 × 20 cm [9¾" × 7⅞"] (inside center section)
Assorted fat quarters or scraps - (appliqué)
Lightweight interfacing - 22 × 61 cm [8⅝" × 24"]
Embroidery floss- lt green, yellow, grey, and black
1 Button - 1 cm [⅜"]
Magnetic button - one pair

❧ Directions
1 Appliqué and embroider the design on the front of the linen; sew on the bottom section so that the watering can touches the bottom section; press the seam allowance toward the bottom section; fuse the lightweight interfacing to the wrong side.

2 Sew the bottom sections to both facings A and B; fuse the lightweight interfacing to the wrong side. Finish the edges that will be showing (Diagram 1).

3 With right sides together, layer facings A, B and the inside center section against the appliquéd cover, matching edges; sew all the way around the edges (Diagram 2).

4 Snip into the curves of facing A to help with ease; turn right side out. Referring to Diagram 3 and the Dimensional Diagram, attach the magnetic button and decorative button.

Dimensional Diagram

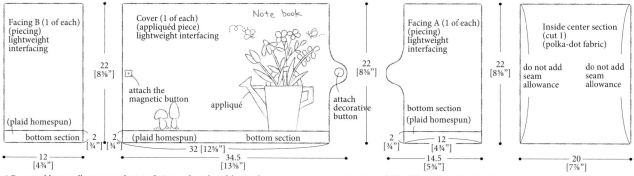

* Do not add seam allowance to the interfacing or the sides of the inside center section; use a 1.2 - 1.5 cm [½" - ⅝"] wide bias binding for the stem appliqué; add 0.3 - 0.5 cm [⅛" -¼"] to the appliqués other than the stem; add 1.5 cm [⅝"] to the facings A and B; add 0.7 cm [¼"] for all else.

Diagram 1

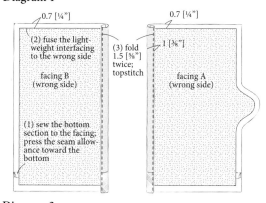

Diagram 3

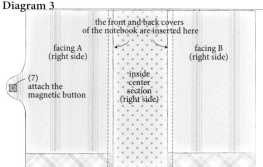

(6) turn right side out and adjust the shape

Diagram 2

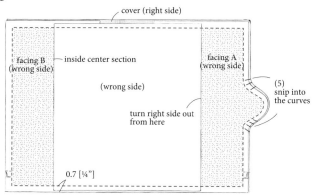

(4) With right sides together, layer facings A, B and the inside center section against the appliquéd cover, matching edges; sew all the way around the edges

❧ Finished measurements
27 cm [10⅝"] (height)
10 × 33 cm [4" × 13"] (bottom)

Dimensional Diagram

❧ Materials
Homespun, two kinds - 50 × 40 cm each [19¾" × 15¾"]
(bag body front, bag body back)
Homespun - 12 × 35 cm [4¾" × 13¾"] (bag bottom top)
Plaid homespun - 90 × 90 cm [35⅜" × 35⅜"]
 (lining, facing, and 2.5 cm [1"] wide bias binding)
Assorted fat quarters or scraps, two kinds - (appliqué)
Batting - 110 × 45 cm [43¼" × 17¾"]
Lightweight interfacing - 24 × 36 cm [9½" × 14⅛"] (facing)
Heavyweight interfacing - 10.5 × 33.5 cm [4⅛" × 13¼"]
 (bag bottom)
Embroidery floss - lt beige

❧ Directions

1 Appliqué and embroider the design on the right section of the bag body front. With right sides together, sew the left and right sections of the bag body front together; press the seam toward the left side. With wrong sides together and batting in between, lay the bag body front and lining together; baste; quilt. Following the same directions, make the bag body back.

2 Cut out the four pattern pieces for the facing. Fuse the lightweight interfacing (no seam allowance) to the wrong side of the facing pieces. Draw the finished sewing line on the wrong side of the quilted bag body front and bag body back. With right sides together and matching center seams, sew the facing pieces to the front and back of the bag body handle areas along the finished sewing lines. Trim the seam allowance down to 0.7 cm [¼"]. Fold the facing to the inside along the seam line; turn the seam allowance under and blindstitch down to the lining.

3 With right sides together, sew the bag body front and bag body back together. Trim the seam allowance down to 0.7 cm [¼"] except for one of the bag back lining; use the lining to bind the raw edges; blindstitch down. Use the 2.5 cm [1"] bias binding to finish the bag opening as you did for the facing.

4 Topstitch the bag opening and handle area.

5 Fuse the heavyweight interfacing to the wrong side of the bag bottom lining (no seam allowance). With wrong sides together and batting in between, baste and quilt the bag bottom.

6 With right sides together, sew the bag bottom and bag body together. Trim the seam allowance down to 0.7 cm [¼"] except for the bag bottom lining; use the lining to bind the raw edges; blindstitch down.

7 With right sides together, sew the handle areas together. Trim the seam allowances down to 0.7 cm [¼"] and press open. Fold the handles in half lengthwise, mark 14 cm [5½"] across, and stitch the handle along the edges by machine.

Bag Body Front /Bag Body Back (2 of each)
Left section top (homespun)
Right section top (appliquéd piece)
batting *
lining * (plaid homespun)

* cut the batting and lining on the fold, so that they are one continuous piece

Facing (2 of each)
(plaid homespun)
lightweight interfacing

18 [7⅛"]

20.3 [8"]

1.5 [⅝"]

18 [7⅛"]

right section

sew the side seams up to the bag opening

sew the side seams up to the bag opening

left section

30.3 [11⅞"]

27 [10⅝"]

30.3 [11⅞"]

outline quilt around the appliqués

quilt following the pattern on the fabric

appliqué

free form quilting

18.6 [7¼"]

18.6 [7¼"]

10.5 [4⅛"]

quilt in a 1 cm [⅜"] grid

Bag Bottom (1 of each)
top (homespun)
batting
lining (plaid homespun)
heavyweight interfacing

33.3 [13¼"]

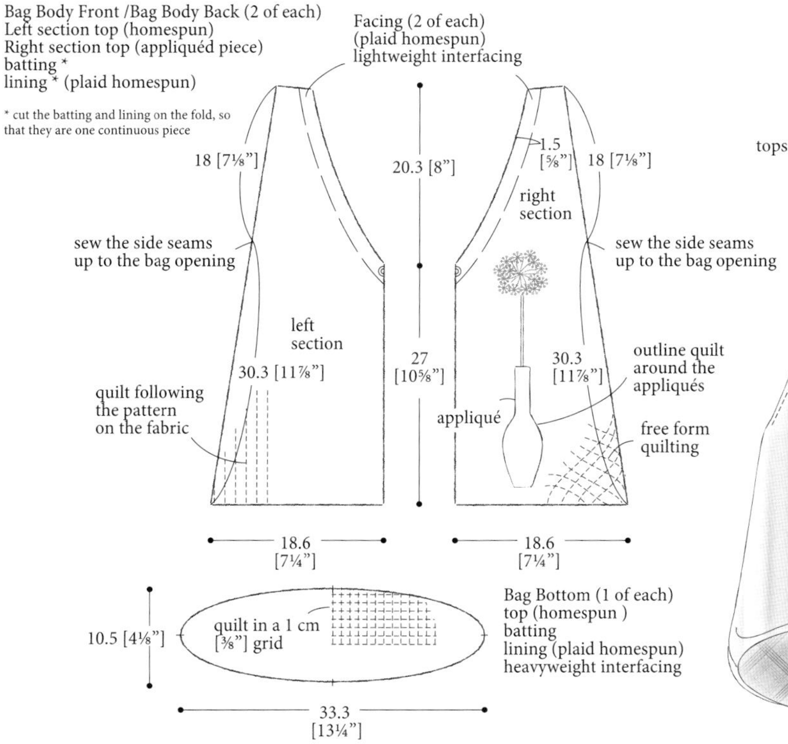

* Do not add any seam allowance to the interfacing; add 3 cm [1¼"] seam allowance to the batting and lining; use a 1.2 - 1.5 cm wide bias binding for the stem appliqué; add 0.3 - 0.5 cm [⅛" - ¼"]seam allowance to all appliqués other than the stem; add 0.7 cm [¼"] for all else.

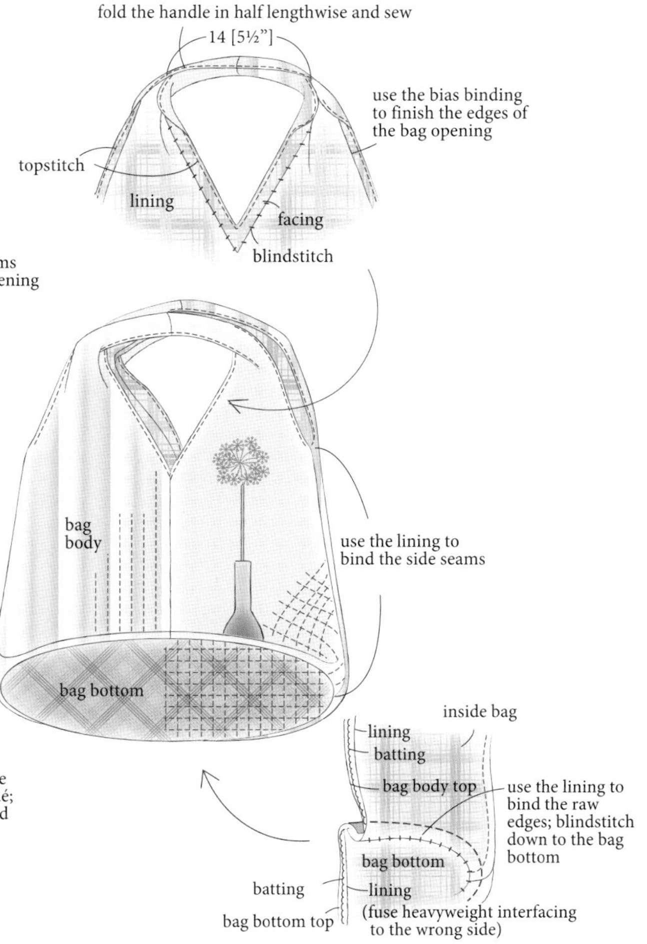

fold the handle in half lengthwise and sew

14 [5½"]

use the bias binding to finish the edges of the bag opening

topstitch

lining

facing

blindstitch

bag body

use the lining to bind the side seams

bag bottom

inside bag

lining

batting

bag body top

use the lining to bind the raw edges; blindstitch down to the bag bottom

batting

bag bottom

lining

bag bottom top

(fuse heavyweight interfacing to the wrong side)

Floral Display Bag

❧ **Materials**
Print - 38 × 50 cm [15" × 19¾"] (bag body front, handle backing)
Print - 28 × 40 cm [11" × 15¾"] (bag body back)
Print - 10 × 80 cm [4" × 31½"] (gusset)
Plaid homespun - 90 × 80 cm [35⅜" × 31½"] (bag lining, gusset lining, 2.5 cm [1"]wide bias fabric)
Assorted fat quarters or scraps - (appliqué)
Plaid homespun - 3.5 × 210 cm [1⅜" × 82¾"] (bias binding for the bag opening and handle)
Batting - 110 × 45 cm [43¼" × 17¾"]
Lightweight interfacing - 26 × 37 cm [10¼" × 14½"] (bag body back)
Medium-weight interfacing - 9 × 38 cm [3½" × 15"] (handle)
Heavyweight interfacing - 7 × 77 cm [2¾" × 30¼"] (gusset)
Beige nylon webbing - 4.5 × 76 cm [1¾" × 29⅞"] (handle)
Embroidery floss - green, grey
4 Wooden buttons - 3 cm [1¼"]

❧ **Finished measurements**
24 × 37 cm [9½" × 14½"]
7 cm [2¾"] (gusset width)

❧ **Directions**
1 Make the bag body front and bag body back following the directions below (Diagram 1 and Diagram 2). Finish the bag opening of the bag using the bias binding to bind the raw edges (Diagram 3).
2 Make the gusset (Diagram 4). With right sides together, sew the bag body front and back and gusset together. Bind the raw edges using the 2.5 cm [1"] wide bias fabric.
3 Make the bag handles following the directions (Diagram 6). Attach the handles to the bag by sewing them in place; sew the decorative buttons on the handles to finish (Diagram 7).

Dimensional Diagram

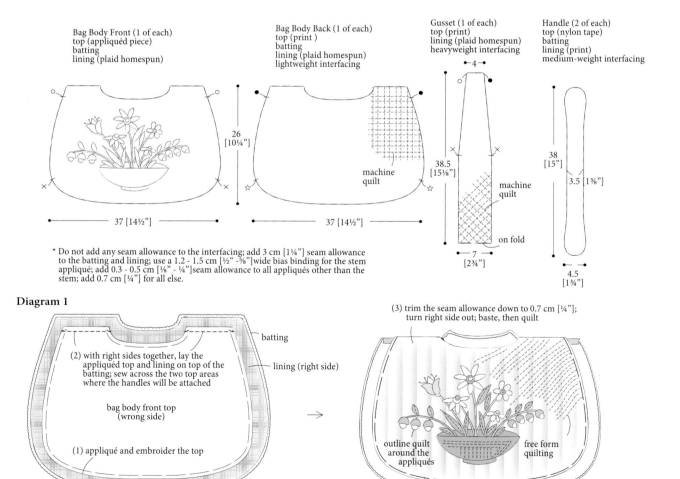

Bag Body Front (1 of each)
top (appliquéd piece)
batting
lining (plaid homespun)

Bag Body Back (1 of each)
top (print)
batting
lining (plaid homespun)
lightweight interfacing

machine quilt

26 [10¼"]

37 [14½"]

37 [14½"]

Gusset (1 of each)
top (print)
lining (plaid homespun)
heavyweight interfacing

4

38.5 [15⅛"]

machine quilt

on fold

7 [2¾"]

Handle (2 of each)
top (nylon tape)
batting
lining (print)
medium-weight interfacing

38 [15"]

3.5 [1⅜"]

4.5 [1¾"]

* Do not add any seam allowance to the interfacing; add 3 cm [1¼"] seam allowance to the batting and lining; use a 1.2 - 1.5 cm [½" -⅝"]wide bias binding for the stem appliqué; add 0.3 - 0.5 cm [⅛" - ¼"]seam allowance to all appliqués other than the stem; add 0.7 cm [¼"] for all else.

Diagram 1

(2) with right sides together, lay the appliquéd top and lining on top of the batting; sew across the two top areas where the handles will be attached

batting

lining (right side)

bag body front top (wrong side)

(1) appliqué and embroider the top

(3) trim the seam allowance down to 0.7 cm [¼"]; turn right side out; baste, then quilt

outline quilt around the appliqués

free form quilting

(4) take all the basting stitches out except for those around the outside edge

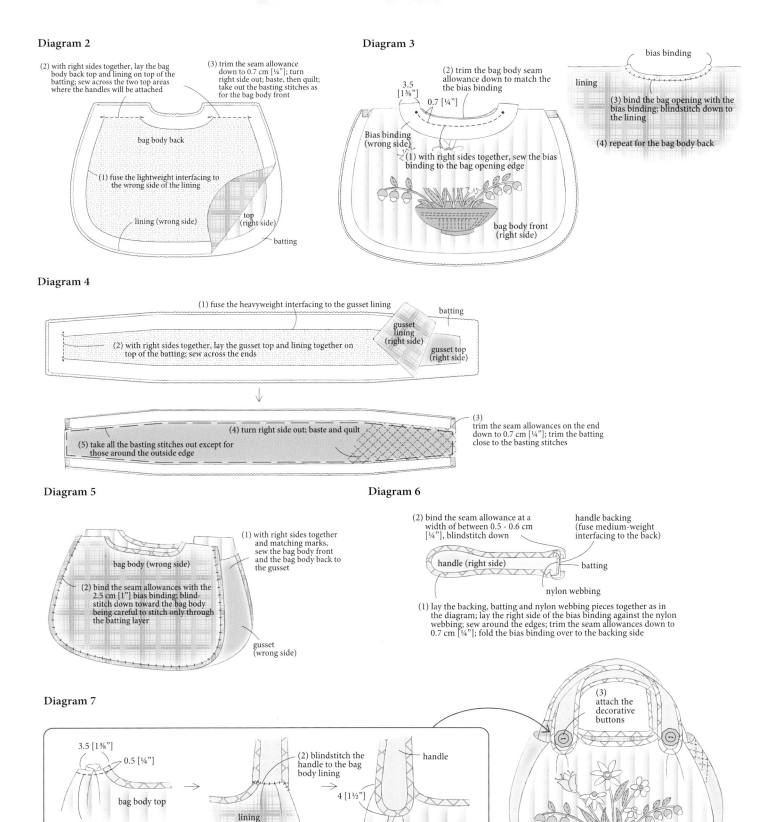

Diagram 2

(2) with right sides together, lay the bag body back top and lining on top of the batting; sew across the two top areas where the handles will be attached

(3) trim the seam allowance down to 0.7 cm [¼"]; turn right side out; baste, then quilt; take out the basting stitches as for the bag body front

bag body back

(1) fuse the lightweight interfacing to the wrong side of the lining

lining (wrong side)

top (right side)

batting

Diagram 3

bias binding

lining

(2) trim the bag body seam allowance down to match the the bias binding

(3) bind the bag opening with the bias binding; blindstitch down to the lining

(4) repeat for the bag body back

3.5 [1⅜"]

0.7 [¼"]

Bias binding (wrong side)

(1) with right sides together, sew the bias binding to the bag opening edge

bag body front (right side)

Diagram 4

(1) fuse the heavyweight interfacing to the gusset lining

batting

gusset lining (right side)

gusset top (right side)

(2) with right sides together, lay the gusset top and lining together on top of the batting; sew across the ends

(4) turn right side out; baste and quilt

(5) take all the basting stitches out except for those around the outside edge

(3) trim the seam allowances on the end down to 0.7 cm [¼"]; trim the batting close to the basting stitches

Diagram 5

(1) with right sides together and matching marks, sew the bag body front and the bag body back to the gusset

bag body (wrong side)

(2) bind the seam allowances with the 2.5 cm [1"] bias binding; blind-stitch down toward the bag body being careful to stitch only through the batting layer

gusset (wrong side)

Diagram 6

(2) bind the seam allowance at a width of between 0.5 - 0.6 cm [¼"], blindstitch down

handle backing (fuse medium-weight interfacing to the back)

handle (right side)

batting

nylon webbing

(1) lay the backing, batting and nylon webbing pieces together as in the diagram; lay the right side of the bias binding against the nylon webbing; sew around the edges; trim the seam allowances down to 0.7 cm [¼"]; fold the bias binding over to the backing side

(3) attach the decorative buttons

Diagram 7

3.5 [1⅜"]

0.5 [¼"]

bag body top

(1) take tucks where the handle will be attached; baste

lining

(2) blindstitch the handle to the bag body lining

handle

4 [1½"]

bag body top

blindstitch underneath the handle end where it will not be visible from the outside

Songbird Mini Tote

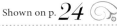

🍂 **Finished measurements**
21 × 32 cm [8¼" × 12⅝"]
8 cm [3⅛"] (gusset width)

🍂 **Materials**
Check homespun A - 110 × 35 cm [43¼" × 13¾"]
   (bag body top, gusset top A, B)
Homespun - 55 × 80 cm [21⅝" × 31½"] (bag body
   lining, gusset lining A and B, 2.5 cm [1"] wide bias
   binding)
Plaid homespun B - 5 × 14 cm [2" × 5½"] (zipper tabs)
Assorted fat quarters or scraps - (appliqué)
Black linen - 11 × 51 cm [4⅜" × 20½"] (handle)
Batting - 55 × 80 cm [21⅝" × 31½"]
Medium-weight interfacing - 21 × 32 cm [8¼" × 12⅝"]
   (bag body back)
Heavyweight interfacing - 15 × 60 cm [5⅞" × 23⅝"]
   (gusset)
Embroidery floss - black, navy blue, green, grey
Sewing thread - brown
1 Zipper - 40 cm [15¾"]
Polka-dot leather strip - 1 × 100 cm [⅜" × 39⅜"]
2 Charms or beads - (zipper pull)

🍂 **Directions**
1 Trace the appliqué design onto the bag body top fabric. Trace and cut out the appliqué pieces. Appliqué the pieces to the top. Layer the bag body top and lining with wrong sides together and batting in between; baste, then quilt.
2 Fuse the medium-weight interfacing to the wrong side of the bag body back. Layer the bag body back and lining with wrong sides together and batting in between; baste, then quilt.
3 Make the two handles (Diagram 1).
4 Make the zipper tabs (Diagram 2).
5 Make gusset A (zipper opening) while referring to Diagram 3, and gusset B (bottom gusset) while referring to Diagram 4.
6 Sew the zipper opening (gusset A) and bottom gusset (gusset B) together, making a cylinder shape. Bind the seams using the 2.5 cm [1"] wide bias fabric (Diagram 5).
7 With right sides together, sew the bag body front, bag body back and the gusset to each other. Trim the seam allowance down to 0.7 cm [¼"] except for the bag body back lining; use the lining to bind the raw edges; blindstitch down.
8 Turn the bag right side out; blindstitch the handle to the bag to secure. Use a Straight Stitch to add decorative visual interest to the ends of the handles (Diagram 6).

Dimensional Diagram

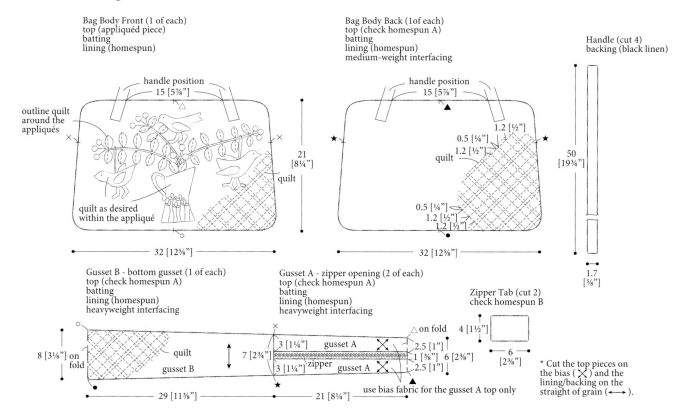

* Do not add any seam allowance to the interfacing pieces; add 0.5 cm [¼"] to the handle, zipper tabs; add 3 cm [1¼"] to the batting, lining; add 1.2 - 1.5 cm [½" - ⅝"] wide bias binding for the stem appliqué; add 0.3 - 0.5 cm [⅛" - ¼"] to the appliqués except the stems; and 0.7 cm [¼"] for all else.

Diagram 1

0.5 [¼"]

(2) turn right side out; fold the ends under 0.5 [¼"]; blindstitch closed on both ends

(3) center the leather strip on the linen; topstitch it to the handle backing (make 2)

(1) with right sides together, sew along the sides lengthwise to make the handle backing

Diagram 2

0.5 [¼"]

on fold

(wrong side)

(1) with right sides together, sew along the side with a 0.5 [¼"] seam allowance

(2) press the seam allowance open

on fold

(right side)

(3) turn right side out; fold in half; baste

Diagram 3

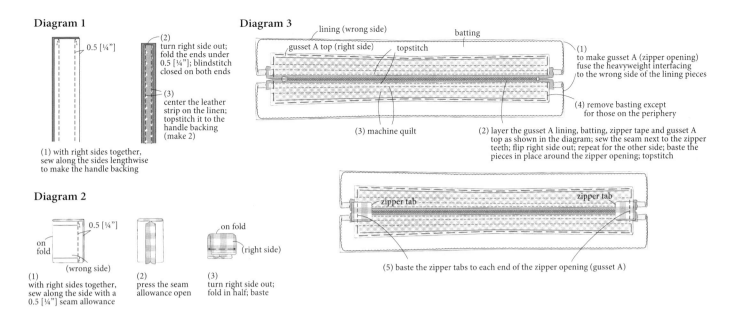

lining (wrong side)   batting

gusset A top (right side)   topstitch

(1) to make gusset A (zipper opening) fuse the heavyweight interfacing to the wrong side of the lining pieces

(4) remove basting except for those on the periphery

(3) machine quilt

(2) layer the gusset A lining, batting, zipper tape and gusset A top as shown in the diagram; sew the seam next to the zipper teeth; flip right side out; repeat for the other side; baste the pieces in place around the zipper opening; topstitch

zipper tab   zipper tab

(5) baste the zipper tabs to each end of the zipper opening (gusset A)

Diagram 4

(2) layer the gusset B lining, batting and top; baste; machine quilt

lining (wrong side)

gusset B top (right side)

(3) take all the basting stitches out except those around the outside edge

batting

(1) fuse the heavyweight interfacing to the wrong side of the lining

Diagram 5

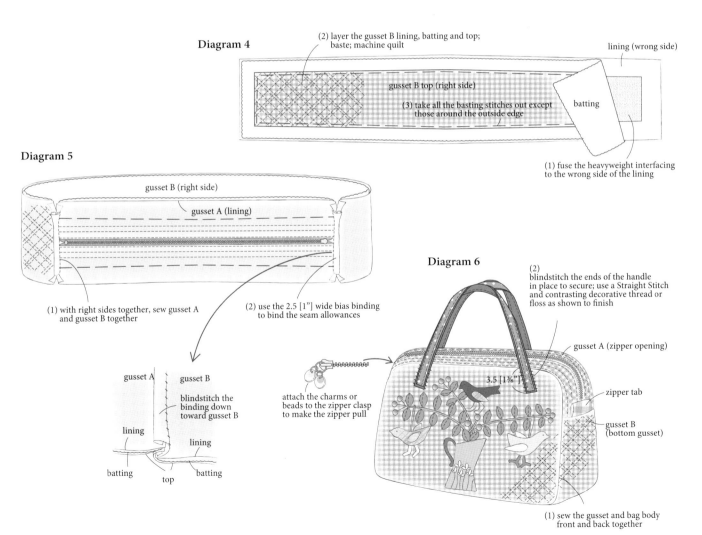

gusset B (right side)

gusset A (lining)

(1) with right sides together, sew gusset A and gusset B together

(2) use the 2.5 [1"] wide bias binding to bind the seam allowances

gusset A   gusset B

blindstitch the binding down toward gusset B

lining   lining

batting   top   batting

attach the charms or beads to the zipper clasp to make the zipper pull

Diagram 6

(2) blindstitch the ends of the handle in place to secure; use a Straight Stitch and contrasting decorative thread or floss as shown to finish

gusset A (zipper opening)

3.5 [1⅜"]

zipper tab

gusset B (bottom gusset)

(1) sew the gusset and bag body front and back together

✻ The full-size template/pattern can be found on Side B of the pattern sheet inserts.

🌿 Finished measurements
21 × 27 cm [8¼" × 10⅝"]
8 cm [3⅛"] (gusset width)

🌿 Materials
Homespun A - 110 × 55 cm [43¼" × 21⅝"] (lining)
Homespun B - 23 × 58 cm [9" × 22⅞"] (pocket top)
Homespun - 10 × 65 cm [4" × 25⅝"] (gusset top)
Polka-dot print - 25 × 60 cm [9¾" × 23⅝"] (bag body back
   top, 2.5 cm [1"] wide bias binding (bag opening)
Assorted fat quarters or scraps - (piecing, appliqué)
Beige print - 22 × 18 cm [8⅝" × 7⅛"]
   (appliqué background)
Plaid homespun - 3.8 × 140 cm [1¾" × 55⅛"] wide bias
   binding
Batting - 41 × 70 cm [16⅛" × 27½"]
Heavyweight interfacing - 30 × 81 cm [11¾" × 31⅞"]
   (bag body back, pockets, and gusset)
Double-sided fusible web - 21 × 54 cm [8¼" × 21¼"]
Embroidery floss - lt beige, lt brown, brown, green
Beige nylon webbing - 2 × 46 cm [¾" × 18⅛"] (handle)
Beige leather tape - 1.5 × 46 cm [⅝" × 18⅛"]
2 Zippers - 25 cm [9¾"]
2 Long beads - 3.5 cm [1⅜"]
2 Round beads - 1 each of two kinds
Waxed cord (grey) - 30 cm [11¾"]

🌿 Directions
1 Make the bag handles (Diagram 1).
2 Make two inner pockets while referring to Diagram 2.
3 Trace the appliqué design onto the bag body top fabric. Trace and cut out the appliqué pieces. Appliqué the pieces to the top. Layer the bag body top and lining with wrong sides together and batting in between; baste, then quilt. Remove all the basting stitches except for those around the outside edge. Use the 2.5 cm [1"] bias binding to bind the zipper opening area at the top (Diagram 3).
4 Fuse the heavyweight interfacing to the wrong side of the bag body back lining. Layer the bag body back and lining with wrong sides together and batting in between; baste, then quilt. Use the 2.5 cm [1"] bias binding to bind the zipper opening area at the top (Diagram 3).
5 To create each zippered pocket for the two sides of the bag, with right sides together, sew one zipper to the bag body front and the one inner pocket (Diagram 4). Repeat for the other side.
6 Make the gusset referring to Diagram 5.
7 Mark the finished sewing line on the bag body pieces. With wrong sides together and aligning edges, pin the bag/pocket front and the bag/pocket back and gusset together; baste. Machine sew them together.
8 Using the 3.8 cm [1¾"] bias binding, sew it with right sides together to the bag side along the finished sewing line. Trim the seam allowance to the edge of the bias binding. Bind the seam allowance and blindstitch down (Diagram 6). Repeat for the other side.
9 Make the zipper pull and attach to the zipper clasp to finish (Diagram 7).

Dimensional Diagram

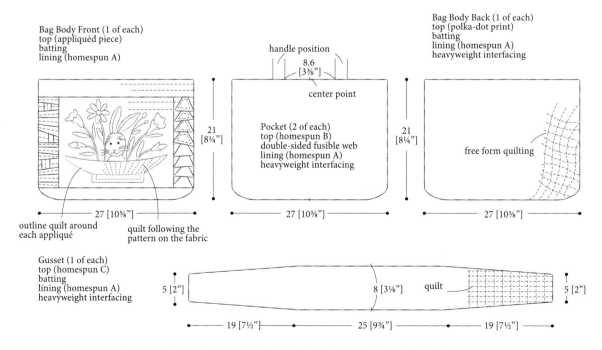

Bag Body Front (1 of each)
top (appliquéd piece)
batting
lining (homespun A)

handle position
8.6 [3⅜"]
center point

Pocket (2 of each)
top (homespun B)
double-sided fusible web
lining (homespun A)
heavyweight interfacing

21 [8¼"]

27 [10⅝"]

outline quilt around each appliqué

quilt following the pattern on the fabric

Bag Body Back (1 of each)
top (polka-dot print)
batting
lining (homespun A)
heavyweight interfacing

21 [8¼"]

free form quilting

27 [10⅝"]

Gusset (1 of each)
top (homespun C)
batting
lining (homespun A)
heavyweight interfacing

5 [2"]

8 [3⅛"]   quilt

5 [2"]

19 [7½"]   25 [9¾"]   19 [7½"]

* Do not add any seam allowance to the interfacing or double-sided fusible web pieces; add 3 cm [1¼"] to the batting, lining; add 1.2 - 1.5 cm [½" - ⅝"] wide bias binding for the stem appliqué; add 0.3 - 0.5 cm [⅛" - ¼"] to the appliqués except the stems; and 0.7 cm [¼"] for all else.

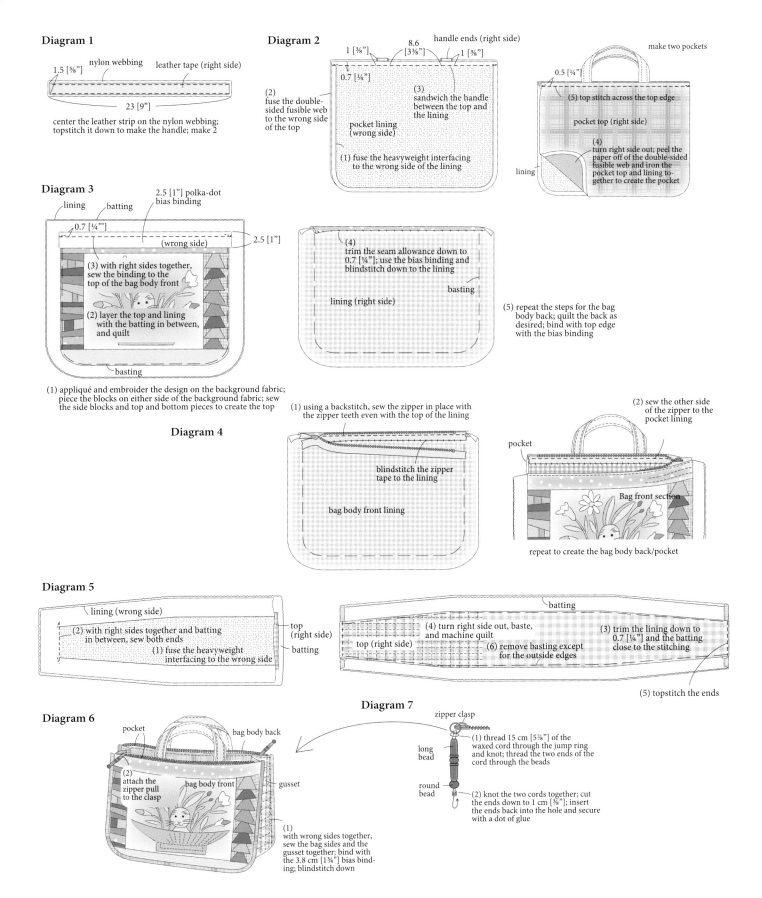

Diagram 1

1.5 [⅝"] nylon webbing leather tape (right side)

23 [9"]

center the leather strip on the nylon webbing; topstitch it down to make the handle; make 2

Diagram 2

8.6 [3⅜"]   handle ends (right side)

1 [⅜"]   1 [⅜"]

0.7 [¼"]

(2) fuse the double-sided fusible web to the wrong side of the top

(3) sandwich the handle between the top and the lining

pocket lining (wrong side)

(1) fuse the heavyweight interfacing to the wrong side of the lining

make two pockets

0.5 [¼"]

(5) top stitch across the top edge

pocket top (right side)

(4) turn right side out; peel the paper off of the double-sided fusible web and iron the pocket top and lining together to create the pocket

lining

Diagram 3

2.5 [1"] polka-dot bias binding

lining   batting

0.7 [¼"]

(wrong side)

2.5 [1"]

(3) with right sides together, sew the binding to the top of the bag body front

(2) layer the top and lining with the batting in between, and quilt

basting

(1) appliqué and embroider the design on the background fabric; piece the blocks on either side of the background fabric; sew the side blocks and top and bottom pieces to create the top

(4) trim the seam allowance down to 0.7 [¼"]; use the bias binding and blindstitch down to the lining

basting

lining (right side)

(5) repeat the steps for the bag body back; quilt the back as desired; bind with top edge with the bias binding

Diagram 4

(1) using a backstitch, sew the zipper in place with the zipper teeth even with the top of the lining

blindstitch the zipper tape to the lining

bag body front lining

(2) sew the other side of the zipper to the pocket lining

pocket

Bag front section

repeat to create the bag body back/pocket

Diagram 5

lining (wrong side)

(2) with right sides together and batting in between, sew both ends

(1) fuse the heavyweight interfacing to the wrong side

top (right side)

batting

batting

(4) turn right side out, baste, and machine quilt

top (right side)

(6) remove basting except for the outside edges

(3) trim the lining down to 0.7 [¼"] and the batting close to the stitching

(5) topstitch the ends

Diagram 6

pocket

bag body back

(2) attach the zipper pull to the clasp

bag body front

gusset

(1) with wrong sides together, sew the bag sides and the gusset together; bind with the 3.8 cm [1¾"] bias binding; blindstitch down

Diagram 7

zipper clasp

long bead

round bead

(1) thread 15 cm [5⅞"] of the waxed cord through the jump ring and knot; thread the two ends of the cord through the beads

(2) knot the two cords together; cut the ends down to 1 cm [⅜"]; insert the ends back into the hole and secure with a dot of glue

★ The full-size template/pattern can be found on Side B of the pattern sheet inserts.

❧ Finished measurements
20 cm [7⅞"] (height)
9.8 cm [3⅞"] (bottom)

❧ Materials

Brown print - 22 × 85 cm [8⅝" × 33½"] (bucket side top/outer)

Grey print - 56 × 56 cm [22" × 22"] (bucket lining)

Brown homespun - 12 × 12 cm [4¾" × 4¾"] (bucket bottom top/outer)

Muslin - 56 × 56 cm [22" × 22"] (facing)

Assorted fat quarters or scraps - (appliqué)

Batting - 56 × 56 cm [22" × 22"]

Fusible batting - 50 × 50 cm [19¾" × 19¾"]

Embroidery floss - yellow-green

Clear template plastic - 40 × 88 cm [15¾" × 34⅝"]

Pom pom ribbon (brown) - 95 cm [37⅜"]

❧ Directions

1 Cut out the fabric pieces for the top/outer, facing and template plastic referring to the dimensional diagram below and the pattern sheet insert. Trace the appliqué design onto the bucket side top/outer pieces. Trace and cut out the appliqué pieces. Appliqué and embroider all four sides. With right sides together, sew the four bucket side top/outer pieces to the bucket bottom top/ outer piece (Diagram 1).

2 With wrong sides together, layer the sewn bucket top/outer and facing with batting in between; baste, quilt. Remove the basting except for those around the outside edges (Diagram 1).

3 Draw the finished sewing line on the facing side and take measurements. Add 3 cm [1¼"] to these measurements as a seam allowance as you cut the lining and the fusible batting. Fuse the batting to the wrong side of the lining.

4 With right sides together, layer the bucket top/outer and lining and sew the together the "v" areas (not the opening edges); trim the seam allowance down to 0.7 cm [¼"] and clip into the inner "v" area (Diagram 2).

5 Turn right side out; using a backstitch, sew the pom pom ribbon to each of the four sides at the opening edge. Sew three sides of the bottom on the seam line, leaving one side open to insert the template plastic (Diagram 3).

6 Cut and insert two pieces of template plastic that will serve as the bottom unstitched side; sew the remaining seam closed securely by hand. Cut out eight pieces of template plastic for the sides; insert two of each into the four sides and blindstitch the openings closed (Diagram 4).

7 Lift the sides up and sew them together using a ladder stitch (Diagram 5).

Dimensional Diagram

* Do not add any seam allowance to the template plastic or the fusible batting; add 3 cm [1¼"] seam allowance to the batting, facing and lining; use a 1.2 - 1.5 cm [½" - ⅝"] wide bias binding for the stem appliqué; add 0.3 - 0.5 cm [⅛" - ¼"] seam allowance to all appliqués other than the stem; add 0.7 cm [¼"] for all else.

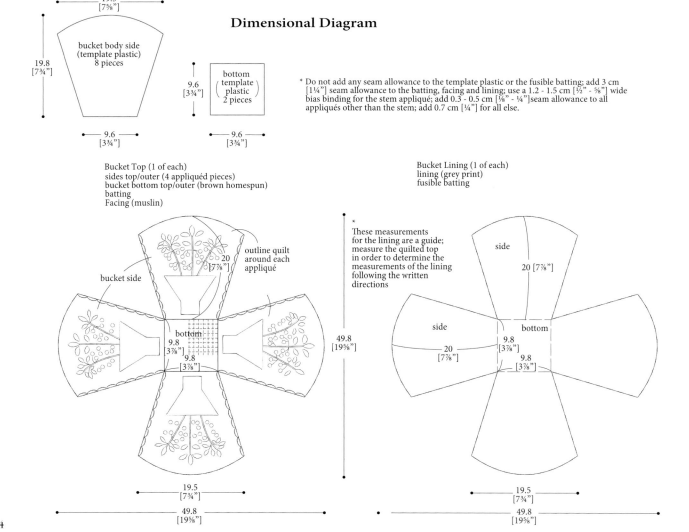

Diagram 1

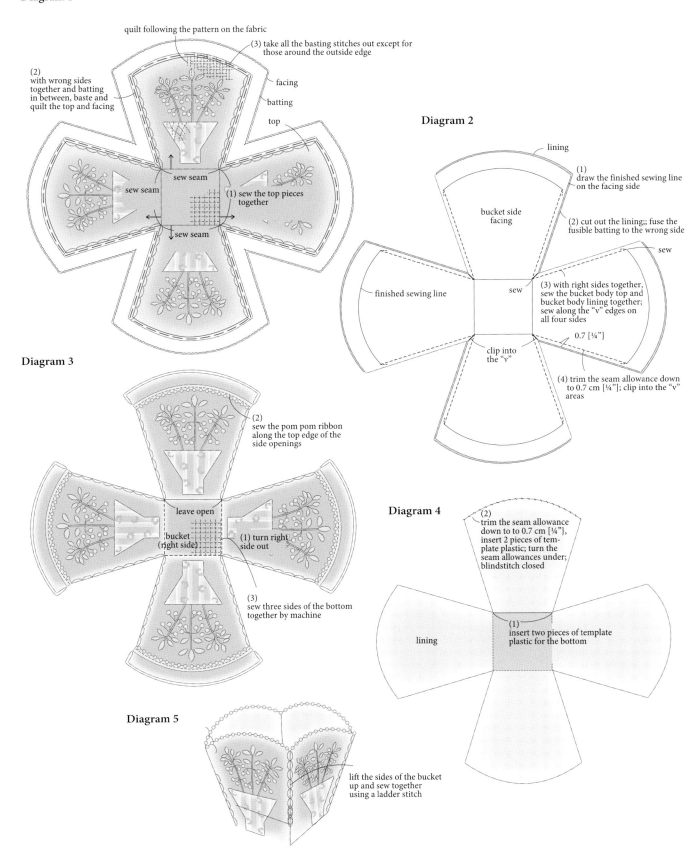

quilt following the pattern on the fabric

(3) take all the basting stitches out except for those around the outside edge

facing

batting

top

(2) with wrong sides together and batting in between, baste and quilt the top and facing

sew seam

sew seam

sew seam

(1) sew the top pieces together

Diagram 2

lining

(1) draw the finished sewing line on the facing side

bucket side facing

(2) cut out the lining;; fuse the fusible batting to the wrong side

sew

sew

finished sewing line

sew

(3) with right sides together, sew the bucket body top and bucket body lining together; sew along the "v" edges on all four sides

0.7 [¼"]

clip into the "v"

(4) trim the seam allowance down to 0.7 cm [¼"]; clip into the "v" areas

Diagram 3

(2) sew the pom pom ribbon along the top edge of the side openings

leave open

bucket (right side)

(1) turn right side out

(3) sew three sides of the bottom together by machine

Diagram 4

(2) trim the seam allowance down to to 0.7 cm [¼"}, insert 2 pieces of template plastic; turn the seam allowances under; blindstitch closed

(1) insert two pieces of template plastic for the bottom

lining

Diagram 5

lift the sides of the bucket up and sew together using a ladder stitch

🌿 Finished measurements
22 × 13 cm [8⅝" × 5⅛"]
4.8 cm [1⅞"] (gusset width)

🌿 Materials

Grey homespun - 35 × 30 cm [13¾" × 11¾"] (case body top, zipper tab)

Print A - 50 × 55 cm [19¾" × 21⅝"] (case lining, gusset lining, pocket A, and 2.5 [1"] bias binding for pocket seams)

Print fabric B - 40 × 40 cm [15¾" × 15¾"] (gusset top, handle backing)

Check homespun - 25 × 25 cm [9¾" × 9¾"] (handle top)

Assorted fat quarters or scraps - (appliqué)

Check homespun - 3.5 × 120 cm [1⅜" × 47¼"] (binding)

Beige mesh/netting - 10 × 24 cm [4" × 9½"] (pocket B)

Batting - 50 × 50 cm [19¾" × 19¾"]

Flannel - 1.5 × 5 cm [⅝" × 2"] (zipper tab)

Medium-weight interfacing - 2.5 × 22 cm [1" × 8⅝"] (handle)

Heavyweight interfacing - 5 × 44 cm [2" × 17¼"] (gusset)

Embroidery floss - pale grey, grey, green

1 Zipper - 43 cm [16⅞"]

1 Zipper - 20 cm [7⅞"]

1 Button - 1.8 cm [⅝"}

🌿 Directions

1 Trace the appliqué design onto the case body top fabric. Trace and cut out the appliqué pieces. Appliqué the pieces to the lid section of the case body top.

2 Layer the case body top and lining with wrong sides together and batting in between; baste, then quilt. Remove all the basting stitches except for those around the outside edge. Draw the finished sewing line on the lining side.

3 Make the handle; sew the handle in position on the gusset by machine (Diagram 1).

4 Make the pocket with the 20 cm [7⅞"] zipper and sew it to the lining side of the case (Diagram 2).

5 Fuse the heavyweight interfacing to the wrong side of the gusset lining. Place the 43 cm [16⅞"] zipper and gusset top right sides together and baste. With right sides together, lay the gusset top against the gusset lining with the batting against the top. Sew on the zipper side.

6 Trim the batting and lining to match the gusset top piece. Turn right side out; press; machine quilt to finish the gusset.

7 With wrong sides together, baste the gusset and case body together. Baste the zipper tape to the case lid.

8 With right sides together, pin the 3.5 cm [1⅜"] bias binding around the edges of the case; machine sew. Trim the seam allowance to the same as the bias binding. Bind the edges; blindstitch down to the lining all the way around the case (Diagram 3).

9 Make the zipper pull out of the fabric and button and attach to the zipper clasp to finish (Diagram 4).

Dimensional Diagram

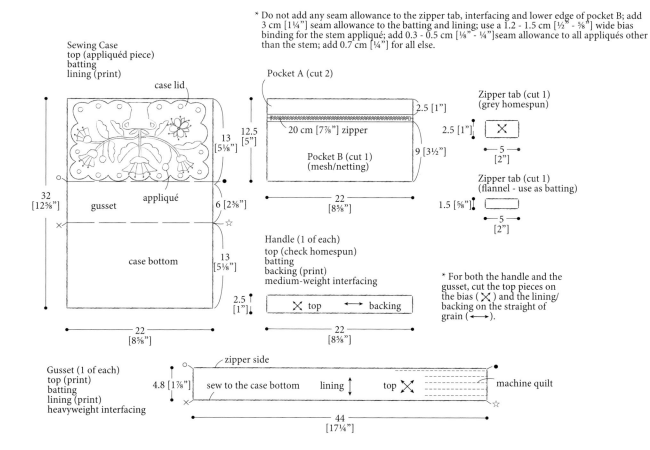

* Do not add any seam allowance to the zipper tab, interfacing and lower edge of pocket B; add 3 cm [1¼"] seam allowance to the batting and lining; use a 1.2 - 1.5 cm [½" - ⅝"] wide bias binding for the stem appliqué; add 0.3 - 0.5 cm [⅛" - ¼"]seam allowance to all appliqués other than the stem; add 0.7 cm [¼"] for all else.

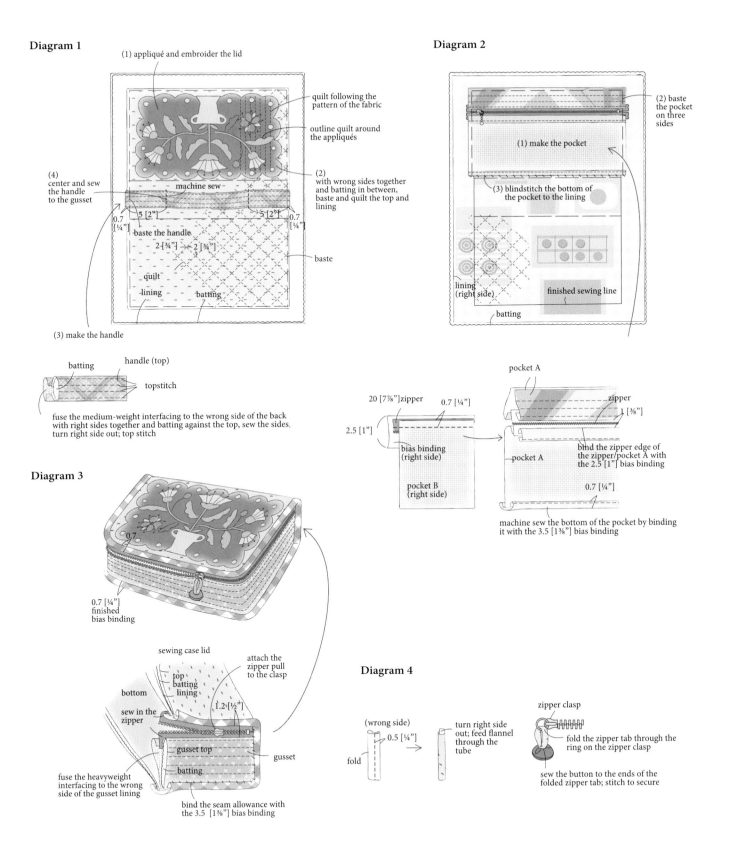

Diagram 1

(1) appliqué and embroider the lid

quilt following the pattern of the fabric

outline quilt around the appliqués

(2) with wrong sides together and batting in between, baste and quilt the top and lining

(4) center and sew the handle to the gusset

machine sew

0.7 [¼"]   5 [2"]   5 [2"]   0.7 [¼"]

baste the handle

2 [¾"]   2 [¾"]

baste

quilt

lining

batting

(3) make the handle

batting

handle (top)

topstitch

fuse the medium-weight interfacing to the wrong side of the back with right sides together and batting against the top, sew the sides, turn right side out; top stitch

Diagram 2

(2) baste the pocket on three sides

(1) make the pocket

(3) blindstitch the bottom of the pocket to the lining

lining (right side)

finished sewing line

batting

20 [7⅞"] zipper   0.7 [¼"]

2.5 [1"]

bias binding (right side)

pocket B (right side)

pocket A

zipper

[⅜"]

bind the zipper edge of the zipper/pocket A with the 2.5 [1"] bias binding

pocket A

0.7 [¼"]

machine sew the bottom of the pocket by binding it with the 3.5 [1⅜"] bias binding

Diagram 3

0.7

0.7 [¼"] finished bias binding

sewing case lid

attach the zipper pull to the clasp

top
batting
lining

bottom

sew in the zipper

1.2 [½"]

gusset top

batting

gusset

fuse the heavyweight interfacing to the wrong side of the gusset lining

bind the seam allowance with the 3.5 [1⅜"] bias binding

Diagram 4

(wrong side)

0.5 [¼"]

fold

turn right side out; feed flannel through the tube

zipper clasp

fold the zipper tab through the ring on the zipper clasp

sew the button to the ends of the folded zipper tab; stitch to secure

Flowers, Birds & Butterflies Wall Hanging ✱ A half-size template/pattern can be found on Side D of the pattern sheet inserts.

⚜ Finished measurements
   99.4 × 86.4 cm [39⅛" × 34"]

⚜ Materials
Assorted fat quarters or scraps - (piecing and appliqué)
2 kinds of homespun - 90 × 15 cm each [35⅜" × 5⅞"] (border A)
2 kinds of homespun - 110 × 15 cm each [43¼" × 5⅞"] (border B)
Print - 110 × 95 cm [43¼" × 37⅜"] (backing)
Check homespun - 3.5 × 375 cm [1⅜" × 147½"] (bias binding)
Batting - 110 × 95 cm [43¼" × 37⅜"]
Embroidery floss - lt beige, lt brown, brown, dk brown, green,
   dk green, greyish-olive, grey, dk grey, charcoal-grey, pink,
   mustard, beige

⚜ Directions
1 Cut out the pieces for the top referring to the dimensional diagram below and the pattern sheet insert. Trace the appliqué design onto the pieced center of the quilt. Trace and cut out the appliqué pieces. Appliqué and embroider the design.
2 Sew border A and border B to the quilt center to finish the quilt top.
3 With wrong sides together and batting in between, layer the quilt top and quilt backing; baste. Machine quilt as desired.
4 Bind the edges using the 3.5 cm [1⅜"] bias binding to finish.

Dimensional Diagram

0.7 [¼"]

binding (check homespun)

Quilt top (1 of each)
appliquéd quilt top
batting
backing (print)

border A

free form quilting

border B

outline quilt around the appliqués and piecing

78 [30¾"]

98 [38½"]

* Add 5 cm [2"] seam allowance to the batting and backing; use a 1.2 - 1.5 cm [½" - ⅝"] wide bias binding for the stem appliqué; add 0.3 - 0.5 cm [⅛" - ¼"] seam allowance to all appliqués other than the stem; add 0.7 cm [¼"] for the piecing and borders

10 [4"]

65 [25⅝"]

10 [4"]

0.7 [¼"]

85 [33½"]

0.7 [¼"]

0.7 [¼"]

Blossom Book Bag

⚜ Materials
Beige print - 25 × 55 cm [9¾" × 21⅝"]
  (appliqué background, pieces "g", "f", "k", and "n")
Dk brown homespun - 40 × 50 cm [15¾" × 19¾"]
  (handle top, handle backing, and bias binding)
Beige homespun - 110 × 37 cm [43¼" × 14½"]
  (bag lining, handle facing)
Brown homespun - 32 × 36 cm [12⅝" × 14⅛"] (bag
  body back top)
Assorted fat quarters or scraps - (piecing and
  appliqué)
Batting - 90 × 40 cm [35⅜" × 15¾"]
Fusible interfacing - 25 × 10 cm [9¾" × 4"]

⚜ Finished measurements
30 × 34 cm [11¾" × 13⅜"]

⚜ Directions
1 Referring to the dimensional diagram and the pattern sheet insert, piece the bag front top and appliqué the design (Diagram 1).
2 With wrong sides together and batting in between, layer the bag body top and lining; baste, then quilt (Diagram 2).
3 Cut the bag body back as a single piece. With wrong sides together and batting in between, layer the bag body back and lining; baste, then machine quilt.
4 Draw the finished sewing line on the lining of the bag body front. With right sides together, sew the sides and bottom by machine (Diagram 3).
5 Trim the seam allowance of the sides/bottom down to 0.7 cm [¼"], except for the lining. Use the lining to bind the raw edges; blindstitch down to the lining (Diagram 3).
6 Make a 3.5 × 75 cm [1⅜" × 29½"] bias binding out of the dk brown homespun; bind the bag opening (Diagram 5).
7 Make the handles (Diagram 4).
8 Referring to Diagram 5, pin the handles to the opening of the bag against the lining; sew to secure, being sure to not stitch through to the top. Cover the handle ends with the handle facing and blindstitch down (Diagram 5).
9 Turn right side out and adjust the shape to finish.

Dimensional Diagram

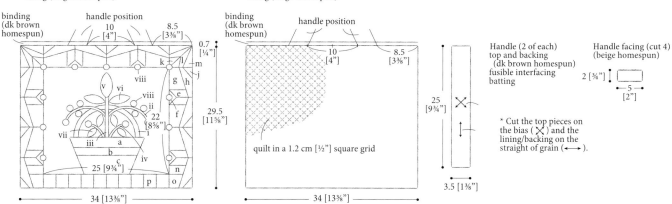

Bag Body Front (1 of each)
top (appliquéd top)
batting
lining (beige homespun)

binding (dk brown homespun)
handle position
10 [4"]
8.5 [3⅜"]
0.7 [¼"]
k l m
j
viii
g h
v vi
viii
e
ii
22 (8⅝")
f
vii
i
iii a
b
c iv
25 [9¾"]
n
p o
29.5 [11⅝"]
34 [13⅜"]

Bag Body Back (1 of each)
top (brown homespun)
batting
lining (beige homespun)

binding (dk brown homespun)
handle position
10 [4"]
8.5 [3⅜"]
quilt in a 1.2 cm [½"] square grid
34 [13⅜"]

Handle (2 of each)
top and backing
(dk brown homespun)
fusible interfacing
batting
25 [9¾"]
3.5 [1⅜"]

* Cut the top pieces on the bias (✕) and the lining/backing on the straight of grain (⟷).

Handle facing (cut 4)
(beige homespun)
2 [¾"]
5 [2"]

* Do not add any seam allowance to the interfacing; add 3 cm [1¼"] seam allowance to the batting and lining; add 0.7 cm [¼"] to the top and piecing fabrics; use a 1.2 - 1.5 cm [½" - ⅝"] wide bias binding for the stem appliqué; add 0.3 - 0.5 cm [⅛" - ¼"] seam allowance to all appliqués other than the stem; add 0.7 cm [¼"] for all else.

Diagram 1

Diagram 2

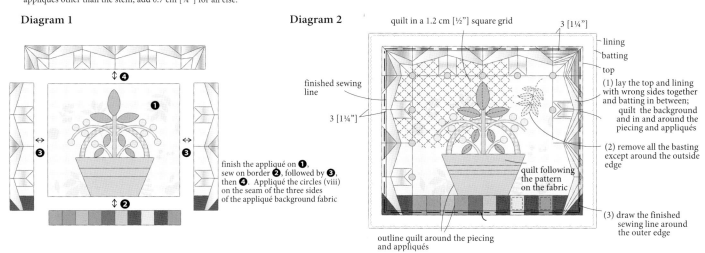

finish the appliqué on ❶, sew on border ❷, followed by ❸, then ❹. Appliqué the circles (viii) on the seam of the three sides of the appliqué background fabric

quilt in a 1.2 cm [½"] square grid
3 [1¼"]
lining
batting
top
(1) lay the top and lining with wrong sides together and batting in between; quilt the background and in and around the piecing and appliqués
finished sewing line
3 [1¼"]
(2) remove all the basting except around the outside edge
quilt following the pattern on the fabric
(3) draw the finished sewing line around the outer edge
outline quilt around the piecing and appliqués

Diagram 3

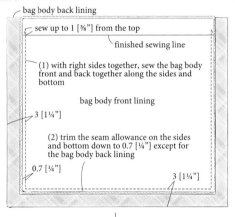

bag body back lining

sew up to 1 [⅜"] from the top

finished sewing line

(1) with right sides together, sew the bag body front and back together along the sides and bottom

bag body front lining

3 [1¼"]

(2) trim the seam allowance on the sides and bottom down to 0.7 [¼"] except for the bag body back lining

0.7 [¼"]

3 [1¼"]

↓ bag body front lining

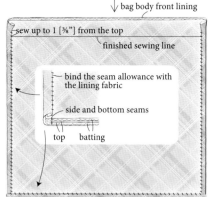

sew up to 1 [⅜"] from the top

finished sewing line

bind the seam allowance with the lining fabric

side and bottom seams

top   batting

Diagram 4

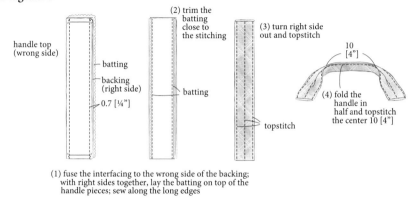

handle top (wrong side)

batting

backing (right side)

0.7 [¼"]

(2) trim the batting close to the stitching

batting

topstitch

(3) turn right side out and topstitch

10 [4"]

(4) fold the handle in half and topstitch the center 10 [4"]

(1) fuse the interfacing to the wrong side of the backing; with right sides together, lay the batting on top of the handle pieces; sew along the long edges

Diagram 5

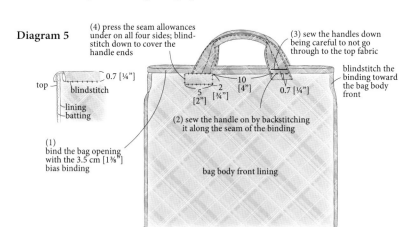

(4) press the seam allowances under on all four sides; blind-stitch down to cover the handle ends

top

0.7 [¼"]

blindstitch

lining
batting

(1) bind the bag opening with the 3.5 cm [1⅜"] bias binding

(3) sew the handles down being careful to not go through to the top fabric

blindstitch the binding toward the bag body front

10 [4"]   2 [¾"]

5 [2"]   0.7 [¼"]

(2) sew the handle on by backstitching it along the seam of the binding

bag body front lining

Shown on p. *41* 🌀 **Daisy Drawstring Bag**

✳ The full-size template/pattern can be found on Side C of the pattern sheet inserts.

⚜ Finished measurements
26 × 24.5 cm [10¼" × 9⅝"]

⚜ Materials

Lt grey print - 26 × 80 cm [10¼" × 31½"] (appliquéd piece)
Green print - 48 × 80 cm [18⅞" × 31½"] (lining)
Blue-grey homespun - 28 × 32 cm [11" × 12⅝"] (handle)
Assorted fat quarters or scraps - (appliqué and drawstring channel)
Plaid homespun - 3.5 × 55 cm [1⅜" × 21⅝"] (binding)
Batting - 48 × 80 cm [18⅞" × 31½"]
Fusible interfacing - 4 × 26 cm [1½" × 10¼"] (handle)
Embroidery floss - white
Brown and grey cording - 0.5 × 82 cm [¼" × 32¼"] (1 of each)
2 Beads - (drawstring)

Dimensional Diagram

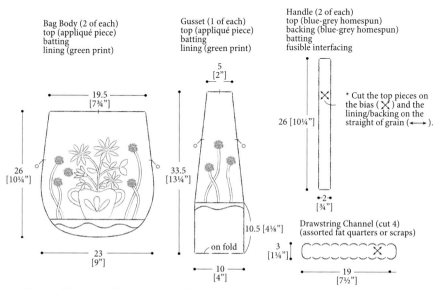

Bag Body (2 of each)
top (appliqué piece)
batting
lining (green print)

Gusset (1 of each)
top (appliqué piece)
batting
lining (green print)

Handle (2 of each)
top (blue-grey homespun)
backing (blue-grey homespun)
batting
fusible interfacing

19.5 [7¾"]

26 [10¼"]

23 [9"]

5 [2"]

33.5 [13¼"]

10.5 [4⅛"]

on fold

10 [4"]

3 [1¼"]

26 [10¼"]

2 [¾"]

* Cut the top pieces on the bias (✕) and the lining/backing on the straight of grain (⟷).

Drawstring Channel (cut 4) (assorted fat quarters or scraps)

19 [7½"]

* Do not add any seam allowance to the interfacing; add 3 cm [1¼"] seam allowance to the batting and lining; use a 1.2 - 1.5 cm [½" - ⅝"] wide bias binding for the stem appliqué; add 0.3 - 0.5 cm [⅛" - ¼"] seam allowance to all appliqués other than the stem; add 0.7 cm [¼"] for all else.

Directions

1 Trace the appliqué design onto the gusset top fabric. Trace and cut out the appliqué pieces. Piece, appliqué, and embroider to make the top fabric of the gusset. With wrong sides together and batting in between; baste, then quilt (Diagram 1).

2 Appliqué and embroider the bag body top/front. With wrong sides together and batting in between, baste, then quilt. Repeat to make the bag back (Diagram 2).

3 Make two each of the handles and drawstring channels referring to Diagram 2 and Diagram 3.

4 Baste the handles to the bag opening. Lay the drawstring channel pieces on top to hide the handle ends. Sew along the long edges to create the channel for the drawstrings. Repeat for the other side (Diagram 4).

5 With wrong sides together, sew the gusset and bag front and back together along the finished sewing lines. Trim the seam allowances to 0.7 cm [¼"] except for the gusset lining. Bind the seam allowances using the lining (Diagram 5).

6 Turn the bag right side out. With right sides together, sew the 3.5 cm [1⅜"] bias binding to the bag opening.

7 Trim the seam allowances to be even with the edge of the bias binding. Bind the raw edges and blindstitch down to the lining (Diagram 6).

8 String the cords from the left and right through the respective drawstring channels. Feed the ends of each cord through the beads (one on each side). Tie the ends of the cords to finish (Diagram 6).

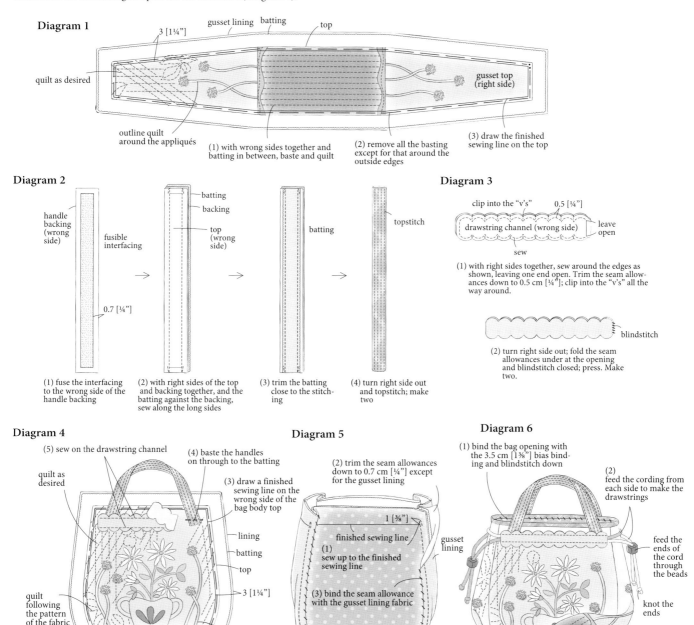

Diagram 1

3 [1¼"] gusset lining batting top

quilt as desired

gusset top (right side)

outline quilt around the appliqués

(1) with wrong sides together and batting in between, baste and quilt

(2) remove all the basting except for that around the outside edges

(3) draw the finished sewing line on the top

Diagram 2

handle backing (wrong side)

fusible interfacing

0.7 [¼"]

batting
backing
top (wrong side)

batting

topstitch

(1) fuse the interfacing to the wrong side of the handle backing

(2) with right sides of the top and backing together, and the batting against the backing, sew along the long sides

(3) trim the batting close to the stitching

(4) turn right side out and topstitch; make two

Diagram 3

clip into the "v's" 0.5 [¼"]

drawstring channel (wrong side)

leave open

sew

(1) with right sides together, sew around the edges as shown, leaving one end open. Trim the seam allowances down to 0.5 cm [¼"]; clip into the "v's" all the way around.

blindstitch

(2) turn right side out; fold the seam allowances under at the opening and blindstitch closed; press. Make two.

Diagram 4

(5) sew on the drawstring channel

(4) baste the handles on through to the batting

quilt as desired

(3) draw a finished sewing line on the wrong side of the bag body top

lining

batting

top

3 [1¼"]

quilt following the pattern of the fabric or as desired

outline quilt around the appliqués

(1) with wrong sides together and batting in between, baste and quilt

(2) remove basting except that around the outside

Diagram 5

(2) trim the seam allowances down to 0.7 cm [¼"] except for the gusset lining

1 [⅜"]

finished sewing line

(1) sew up to the finished sewing line

(3) bind the seam allowance with the gusset lining fabric

gusset lining

bag body lining

Diagram 6

(1) bind the bag opening with the 3.5 cm [1⅜"] bias binding and blindstitch down

(2) feed the cording from each side to make the drawstrings

gusset lining

feed the ends of the cord through the beads

knot the ends

Botanical Cushion Cover ✽ The full-size template/pattern can be found on Side C of the pattern sheet inserts.

🌿 Finished measurements
31 × 42.5 cm [12¼" × 16¾"]

🌿 Materials
Beige print - 28 × 35 cm [11" × 13¾"]
  (piece "m")
Grey homespun - 110 × 50 cm [43¼" × 19¾"]
  (pieces d, f, g, i, j, l, and backing)
Light grey print fabric - 23 × 50 cm [9" × 19¾"]
  (pieces e, h, k, n)
Assorted fat quarters or scraps - (appliqué)
Muslin - 72 × 90 cm [28⅜" × 35⅜"]
  (facing and inner cushion case)
Batting - 37 × 50 cm [14½" × 19¾"]
Embroidery floss - khaki, lt green,
  dk green, grey
Polyester filling - as needed

🌿 Directions
1 Piece the cushion cover front and trace the appliqué design onto it. Trace and cut out the appliqué pieces. Appliqué, and embroider to make the top.
2 With wrong sides together and batting in between, baste, then quilt the cushion cover top and the facing (Diagram 1). Remove the basting except for that around the edges to finish the top of the cushion cover.
3 Cut the cushion cover back in 2 pieces; with wrong sides together, fold each in half. Overlap the folded edges of both pieces in the middle by 7 cm [2¾"] and baste.
4 Lay the cushion cover top and cushion cover back with right sides together; sew around the entire outer edge. Trim the seam allowances to down to 0.7 cm [¼"] except for the facing.
5 Use the facing seam allowance to bind the raw edges (Diagram 2). Turn the cushion cover right side out.
6 To make the inner cushion, with right sides together, sew the muslin together leaving an opening. Turn it right side out and stuff with polyester filling to the desired amount. Blindstitch the opening closed. Stuff the cushion inside the cushion cover to finish.

Dimensional Diagram

* Add 1 cm [⅜"] seam allowance to the cushion cover back and inner cushion case; add 3 cm [1¼"] to the batting and facing; add 0.5 cm [¼"] to the handle, zipper tabs; add 1.2 - 1.5 cm [½" - ⅝"] wide bias binding for the stem appliqué; add 0.3 - 0.5 cm [⅛" - ¼"] to the appliqués except the stems; and 0.7 cm [¼"] for all else.

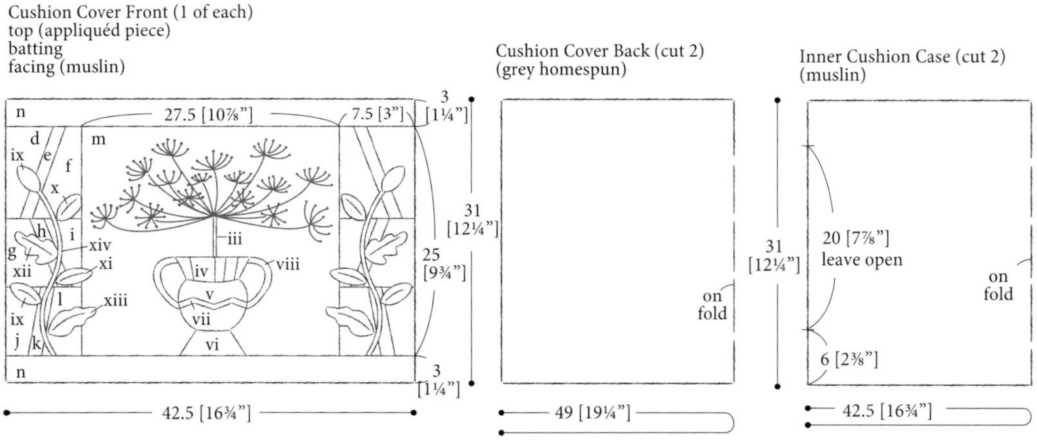

Cushion Cover Front (1 of each)
top (appliquéd piece)
batting
facing (muslin)

n   27.5 [10⅞"]   7.5 [3"]
d / e / f / m
ix / x / i / xiv
h
g / xi
xii / l
ix / j / k / xiii
iii / viii / iv / v / vii / vi
n
3 [1¼"]
31 [12¼"]
25 [9¾"]
3 [1¼"]
42.5 [16¾"]

Cushion Cover Back (cut 2)
(grey homespun)
on fold
31 [12¼"]
49 [19¼"]

Inner Cushion Case (cut 2)
(muslin)
20 [7⅞"] leave open
on fold
31 [12¼"]
6 [2⅜"]
42.5 [16¾"]

Diagram 1

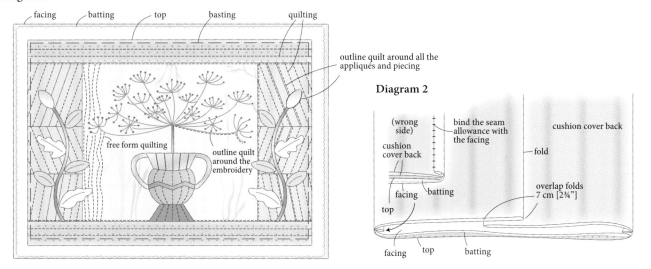

facing — batting — top — basting — quilting

outline quilt around all the appliqués and piecing

free form quilting

outline quilt around the embroidery

Diagram 2

(wrong side)
bind the seam allowance with the facing
cushion cover back
cushion cover back
fold
facing
batting
top
overlap folds 7 cm [2¾"]
facing — top — batting

❧ Finished measurements
15.5 × 30 cm [6⅛" × 11¾"]
when opened up

❧ Materials
Beige homespun - 20 × 55 cm [7⅞" × 21⅝"]
  (appliqué background fabric, pieces a, c, d)
Beige print - 18 × 40 cm [7⅛" × 15¾"] (lining)
Assorted fat quarters or scraps - (piecing, appliqué)
Grey homespun - 3.5 × 17 cm [1⅜" × 6"] (binding)
Embroidery floss - white, mustard
Beige ribbon - 1.5 × 18 cm [⅝" × 7⅛"] (band)
Lt beige cording - 20 cm (book marker)
1 Decorative bead/charm - (end of book marker)

❧ Directions
1 Cut out the fabric pieces for the book cover referring to the dimensional diagram and the pattern sheet insert.
2 Piece, appliqué and embroider the appliqué background fabric (block A). The pieced basket appliqué section becomes the pocket for the book cover, while the appliquéd basket itself becomes a little pocket for putting things in. Do not blindstitch down the top of the little basket, just the sides when you stitch it down (Diagram 1).
3 Piece block B and block C. Trim the seam allowances of the small pieces down to 0.5 cm [¼"], but leave the seam allowance of the outer edges of the overall block at 0.7 cm [¼"] (Diagram 1).
4 Sew block B and block C to block A; press the seam allowance toward blocks B and C to finish the book cover top.
5 Baste the ribbon for the band (that holds the pages in place) and cording just to the outside of the finished sewing line on the right side of the book cover top. Then, with right sides together, lay the book cover top and lining together. Sew around the edges on the finished sewing line, leaving the side open for turning right side out (Diagram 2).
6 Turn it right side out; press. Bind the raw edge with the binding. To finish, fold the book pocket with wrong sides together to the inside; whipstitch across the top and bottom (Diagram 3). Attach the decorative bead or charm to the end of the book mark.

Full-size template of the border pieces

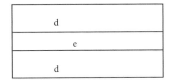

Dimensional Diagram

* Use 1 cm [⅜"]wide bias binding for the stem appliqué; add 0.3 - 0.5 cm [⅛" - ¼"] to the appliqués except the stems; and 0.7 cm [¼"] for all else.

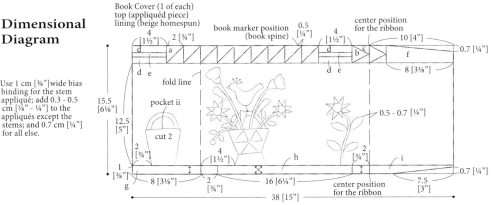

Diagram 1

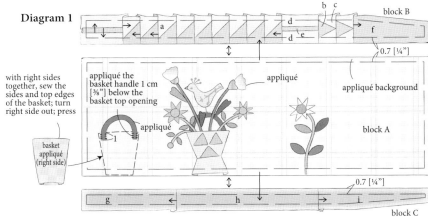

Diagram 2

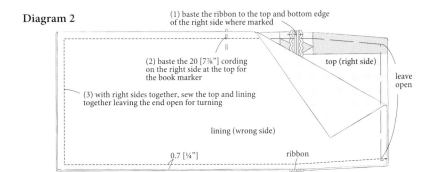

Diagram 3

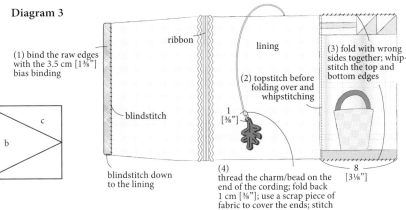

93

Modern Floral Pouch ✳ The full-size template/pattern can be found on Side C of the pattern sheet inserts.

❦ Finished measurements
21.5 × 11.5 cm [8½" × 4½"]
5 cm [2"] (gusset width)

❦ Materials
Green homespun - 25 × 35 cm [9¾" × 13¾"] (piece a)
Brown print - 6 × 35 cm [2⅜" × 13¾"] (piece b)
Brown homespun - 33 × 40 cm [13" × 15¾"] (lining,
gusset bias binding)
Beige homespun -
5 × 23 cm [2" × 9"] (handle top on bias)
3.5 × 37 cm [1⅜" × 14½"] (pouch opening binding)
Blue-grey homespun -
5 × 23 cm [2" × 9"] (handle backing on straight of grain)
3.5 × 37 cm [1⅜" × 14½"] (pouch opening binding)
Homespun - 3 × 47 cm [1¼" × 18½"] (handle binding)
Assorted fat quarters or scraps - (appliqué)
Batting - 33 × 45 cm [13" × 17¾"]
Fusible interfacing - 21 × 3 cm [8¼" × 1¼"]
Embroidery floss - green, lt green, lt beige
1 Zipper - 23 cm [9"]
2 Beads - 1.8 cm [⅝"]
Green waxed cord - 15 cm [5⅞"]
1 Button - 2.5 cm [1"]

❦ Directions

1 Cut out the pattern pieces referring to the dimensional diagram and pattern sheet inserts; trace the appliqué design onto it. Trace and cut out the appliqué pieces. Appliqué, and embroider piece a. Sew to piece b to complete the top; press the seam allowance toward piece b.

2 With wrong sides together and batting in between, baste, then quilt the top. Bind the curved edge with the 3.5 cm [1⅜"] bias binding (Diagram 1).

3 With right sides together, fold the pouch together; sew in the zipper. Then whipstitch the edges of the opening binding together from the end of the zipper to the bottom edge of the pouch (Diagram 2-[1]).

4 Sew the bottom seam; trim the seam allowance down to 0.7 [¼"] except for one of the linings. Use the lining to bind the seam allowance (Diagram 2-[3]). Create the gusset by referring to Diagram 3; use the 2.5 [1"] bias binding to bind the two gusset ends.

5 Make the handle for the pouch referring to Diagram 4.

6 Turn the pouch right side out. Flatten the top of the pouch with the zipper centered and sew across the tip. Sandwich the tip of the bag between the ends of the handle. Sew the handle ends to secure. Make the zipper pull and attach to the zipper clasp to finish the pouch (Diagram 5).

Dimensional Diagram

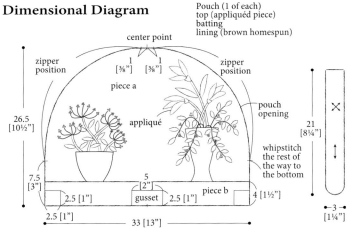

Pouch (1 of each)
top (appliquéd piece)
batting
lining (brown homespun)

center point
zipper position
1 [⅜"] 1 [⅜"]
piece a
zipper position
pouch opening
appliqué
whipstitch the rest of the way to the bottom
26.5 [10½"]
7.5 [3"]
2.5 [1"]
gusset
2.5 [1"]
piece b
4 [1½"]
2.5 [1"]
5 [2"]
33 [13"]

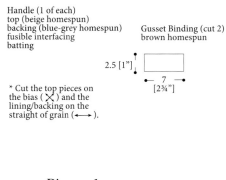

Handle (1 of each)
top (beige homespun)
backing (blue-grey homespun)
fusible interfacing
batting

21 [8¼"]
✳ Cut the top pieces on the bias (✕) and the lining/backing on the straight of grain (⟷).
3 [1¼"]

Gusset Binding (cut 2)
brown homespun
2.5 [1"]
7 [2¾"]

✳ Do not add seam allowance to the fusible interfacing; add 3 cm [1¼"] to the batting and lining; add 0.5 cm [¼"] to the handle, zipper tabs; add 1.2 - 1.5 cm [½" - ⅝"] wide bias binding for the stem appliqué; add 0.3 - 0.5 cm [⅛" - ¼"] to the appliqués except the stems; and 0.7 cm [¼"] to pieces a and b.

Diagram 1

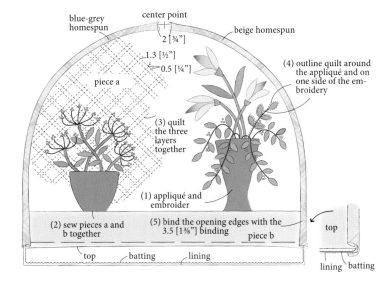

blue-grey homespun
center point
2 [¾"]
1.3 [½"]
0.5 [¼"]
beige homespun
piece a
(4) outline quilt around the appliqué and on one side of the embroidery
(3) quilt the three layers together
(1) appliqué and embroider
(2) sew pieces a and b together
(5) bind the opening edges with the 3.5 [1⅜"] binding
piece b
top batting lining
top
lining batting

Diagram 2

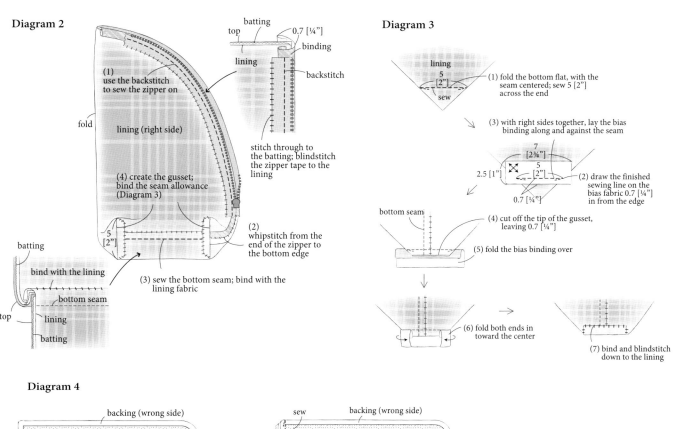

batting

top

0.7 [¼"]

binding

lining

backstitch

(1) use the backstitch to sew the zipper on

fold

lining (right side)

stitch through to the batting; blindstitch the zipper tape to the lining

(4) create the gusset; bind the seam allowance (Diagram 3)

(2) whipstitch from the end of the zipper to the bottom edge

batting

bind with the lining

bottom seam

top

lining

batting

5 [2"]

(3) sew the bottom seam; bind with the lining fabric

Diagram 3

lining

5 [2"]

sew

(1) fold the bottom flat, with the seam centered; sew 5 [2"] across the end

(3) with right sides together, lay the bias binding along and against the seam

7 [2¾"]

5 [2"]

2.5 [1"]

0.7 [¼"]

(2) draw the finished sewing line on the bias fabric 0.7 [¼"] in from the edge

bottom seam

(4) cut off the tip of the gusset, leaving 0.7 [¼"]

(5) fold the bias binding over

(6) fold both ends in toward the center

(7) bind and blindstitch down to the lining

Diagram 4

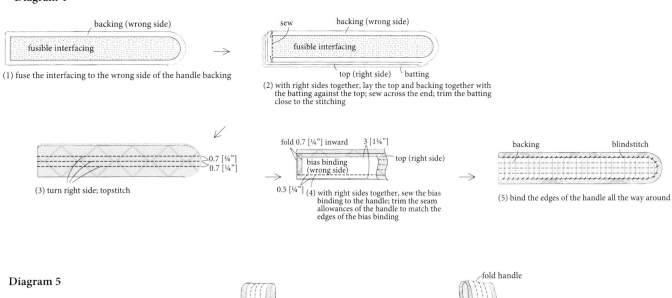

backing (wrong side)

fusible interfacing

(1) fuse the interfacing to the wrong side of the handle backing

sew

backing (wrong side)

fusible interfacing

top (right side)   batting

(2) with right sides together, lay the top and backing together with the batting against the top; sew across the end; trim the batting close to the stitching

0.7 [¼"]
0.7 [¼"]

(3) turn right side; topstitch

fold 0.7 [¼"] inward   3 [1¼"]

bias binding (wrong side)

top (right side)

0.5 [¼"]

(4) with right sides together, sew the bias binding to the handle; trim the seam allowances of the handle to match the edges of the bias binding

backing   blindstitch

(5) bind the edges of the handle all the way around

Diagram 5

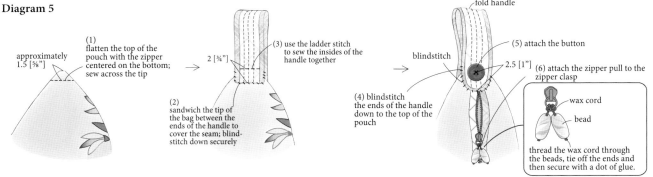

approximately 1.5 [⅝"]

(1) flatten the top of the pouch with the zipper centered on the bottom; sew across the tip

2 [¾"]

(3) use the ladder stitch to sew the insides of the handle together

(2) sandwich the tip of the bag between the ends of the handle to cover the seam; blindstitch down securely

fold handle

blindstitch

(4) blindstitch the ends of the handle down to the top of the pouch

(5) attach the button

2.5 [1"]

(6) attach the zipper pull to the zipper clasp

wax cord

bead

thread the wax cord through the beads, tie off the ends and then secure with a dot of glue.

Shown on p. 44

Pomegranate Shoulder Bag

⁎ The full-size template/pattern can be found on Side C of the pattern sheet inserts.

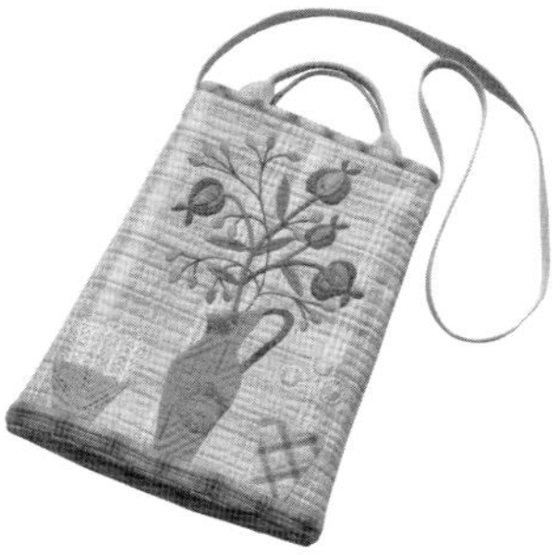

Finished measurements

32 cm [12⅝"] height
24 cm [9½"] bag opening
10 × 25.5 cm [4" × 10"] (bottom)

Materials

Homespun a - 32 × 33 cm [12⅝" × 13"] (bag front piece A)
Homespun b - 32 × 33 cm [12⅝" × 13"] (bag back piece A)
Homespun c - 20 × 33 cm [7⅞" × 13"] (piece B, bottom top)
Homespun d - 110 × 40 cm [43¼" × 15¾"] (bias binding for lining, bottom)
Assorted fat quarters or scraps - (appliqués)
Homespun e - 3.5 × 55 cm [1⅜" × 21⅝"] (bias binding for bag opening)
Batting - 100 × 38 cm [39⅜" × 15"]
Fusible interfacing - 32 × 31 cm [12⅝" × 12¼"] (bag back)
Heavyweight fusible interfacing - 10 × 26 cm [4" × 10¼"] (bottom)
Embroidery floss - brown, lt green, white
Beige cotton webbing - 2.5 × 170 cm [1" × 67"] (handles and shoulder strap)

Directions

1 Appliqué and embroider piece A to make the bag front top. Sew piece B to the lower edge of piece A; press seam allowance toward piece B. With wrong sides together, layer the top and lining with batting in between; baste; quilt as shown (Diagram 1).
2 Piece the bag back top; press seam allowance toward piece B. Fuse the interfacing to the bag back. With wrong sides together, layer the top and lining with batting in between; baste; machine quilt as shown (Diagram 2).
3 With right sides together, layer the bag front and bag back; sew the side seams. Trim the seam allowance down to 0.7 cm [¼"] except for the bag back lining. Use the lining to bind the seam allowance; fold toward the front; blindstitch down to the lining, catching the stitches in the batting (Diagram 3).
4 Make the bag bottom by referring to Diagram 4.
5 With right sides together, pin the bag bottom to the bottom edges of the bag body; sew along the finished sewing line (Diagram 5).
6 Cut a bias strip 2.5 × 65 cm [1" × 25⅝"] from the homespun d fabric. With right sides together, pin the bias binding to the lower edge of the bag (Diagram 6). Trim the excess seam allowance to match the edge of the bias strip. Bind the raw edges; press toward the bottom, and blindstitch down (Diagram 7).
7 Cut the cotton webbing to 23 cm [9"] (adjust the length as desired). Make two. Make handles by referring to Diagram 8. Bind the bag opening and attach the handle (Diagram 9).
8 Cut the desired length for the shoulder strap; sew it to the sides of the bag (Diagram 10).

Dimensional Diagram

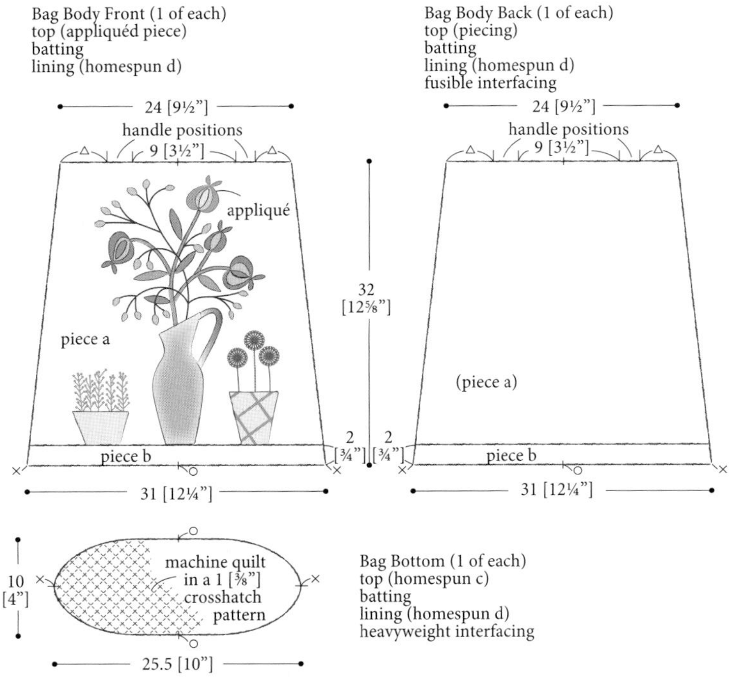
Bag Body Front (1 of each)
top (appliquéd piece)
batting
lining (homespun d)
24 [9½"]
handle positions
9 [3½"]
appliqué
piece a
piece b
2 [¾"]
31 [12¼"]
Bag Body Back (1 of each)
top (piecing)
batting
lining (homespun d)
fusible interfacing
24 [9½"]
handle positions
9 [3½"]
32 [12⅝"]
(piece a)
2 [¾"]
piece b
31 [12¼"]
10 [4"]
machine quilt in a 1 [⅜"] crosshatch pattern
25.5 [10"]
Bag Bottom (1 of each)
top (homespun c)
batting
lining (homespun d)
heavyweight interfacing

* Do not add any seam allowance to the interfacing; add 3 cm [1¼"] seam allowance to the batting and lining; use a 1.2 - 1.5 cm [½" - ⅝"] wide bias binding for the stem appliqué; add 0.3 - 0.5 cm [⅛" - ¼"] seam allowance to all appliqués other than the stem; add 0.7 cm [¼"] for all else.

Diagram 1

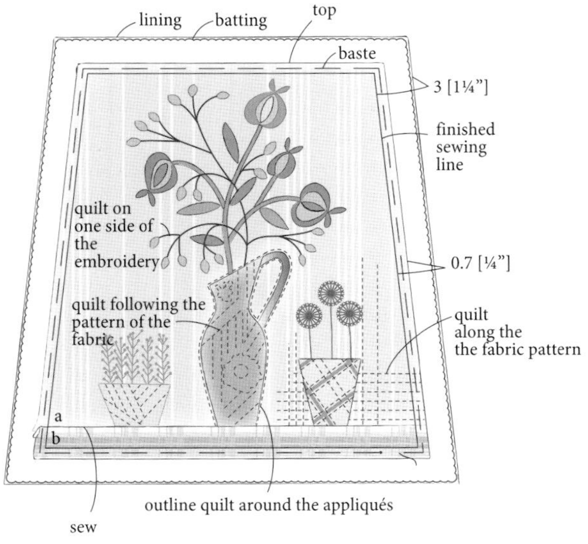
lining
batting
top
baste
3 [1¼"]
finished sewing line
quilt on one side of the embroidery
0.7 [¼"]
quilt following the pattern of the fabric
quilt along the the fabric pattern
a
b
outline quilt around the appliqués
sew

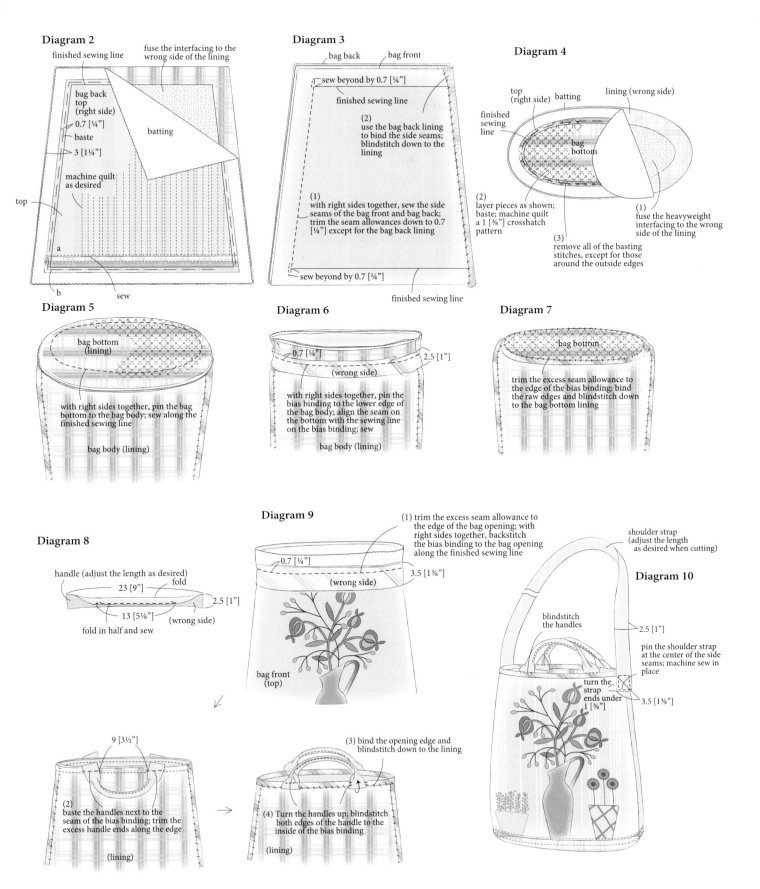

Diagram 2

finished sewing line

fuse the interfacing to the wrong side of the lining

bag back top (right side)

0.7 [¼"]

baste

3 [1¼"]

batting

machine quilt as desired

top

a

b   sew

Diagram 3

bag back   bag front

sew beyond by 0.7 [¼"]

finished sewing line

(2) use the bag back lining to bind the side seams; blindstitch down to the lining

(1) with right sides together, sew the side seams of the bag front and bag back; trim the seam allowances down to 0.7 [¼"] except for the bag back lining

sew beyond by 0.7 [¼"]

finished sewing line

Diagram 4

top (right side)   batting   lining (wrong side)

finished sewing line

bag bottom

(2) layer pieces as shown; baste; machine quilt a 1 [⅜"] crosshatch pattern

(1) fuse the heavyweight interfacing to the wrong side of the lining

(3) remove all of the basting stitches, except for those around the outside edges

Diagram 5

bag bottom (lining)

with right sides together, pin the bag bottom to the bag body; sew along the finished sewing line

bag body (lining)

Diagram 6

0.7 [¼"]   2.5 [1"]

(wrong side)

with right sides together, pin the bias binding to the lower edge of the bag body; align the seam on the bottom with the sewing line on the bias binding; sew

bag body (lining)

Diagram 7

bag bottom

trim the excess seam allowance to the edge of the bias binding; bind the raw edges and blindstitch down to the bag bottom lining

Diagram 8

handle (adjust the length as desired)

23 [9"]   fold

2.5 [1"]

13 [5⅛"]   (wrong side)

fold in half and sew

Diagram 9

(1) trim the excess seam allowance to the edge of the bag opening; with right sides together, backstitch the bias binding to the bag opening along the finished sewing line

0.7 [¼"]   3.5 [1⅜"]

(wrong side)

bag front (top)

9 [3½"]

(2) baste the handles next to the seam of the bias binding; trim the excess handle ends along the edge

(lining)

(3) bind the opening edge and blindstitch down to the lining

(4) Turn the handles up; blindstitch both edges of the handle to the inside of the bias binding

(lining)

Diagram 10

shoulder strap (adjust the length as desired when cutting)

blindstitch the handles

2.5 [1"]

pin the shoulder strap at the center of the side seams; machine sew in place

turn the strap ends under 1 [⅜"]

3.5 [1⅜"]

97

Dimensional Diagram

Pouch (1 of each)
top (appliquéd piece)
batting
lining (beige homespun)

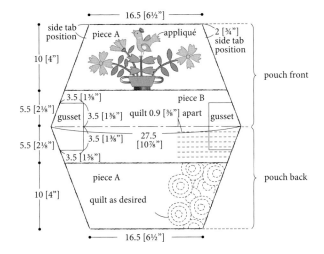

❧ Finished measurements
12.5 × 16.5 cm [5" × 6½"]
7 cm [2¾"] (gusset width)

❧ Materials
Grey print - 12 × 50 cm [4¾" × 19¾"] (piece A)
Dk beige homespun - 13 × 30 cm [5⅛" × 11¾"] (piece B)
Assorted fat quarters or scraps - (appliqués)
Beige homespun - 37 × 40 cm [14½" × 15¾"] (lining, bias binding
  for gusset, zipper tabs; 3.5 × 35 cm [1⅜" × 13¾"] binding for
  pouch opening)
Batting - 37 × 34 cm [14½" × 13⅜"]
Linen ribbon- 1 × 15 cm [⅜" × 5⅞"] (side tabs)
Embroidery floss - mustard yellow, pink, black, lt beige
1 Zipper - 15 cm [5⅞"]
1 Bead - 1.4 cm [½"]
1 Bead - 0.8 cm [⅜"]
Grey waxed cord - 20 cm [7⅞"]

Zipper Tabs (cut 2)
(beige homespun)
4.2 [1⅝"] / 2.5 [1"] / no seam allowance

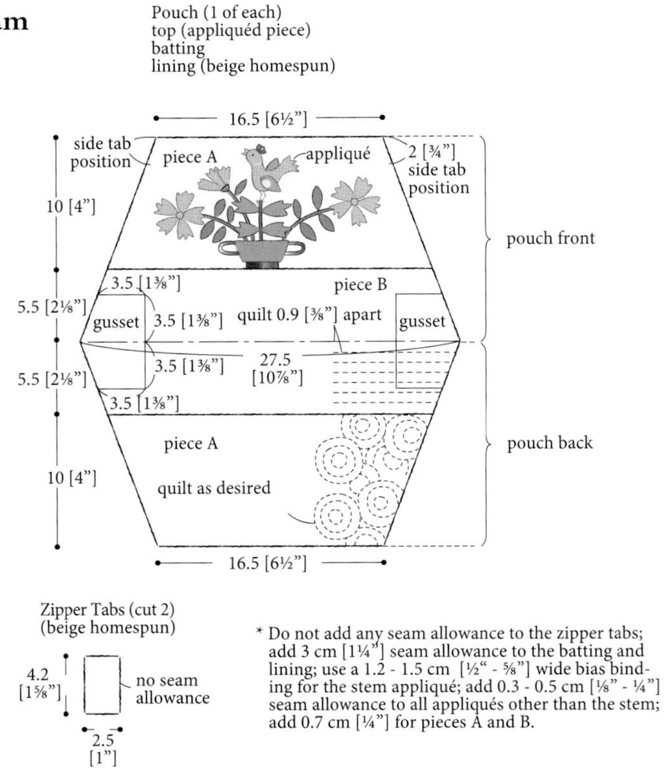

* Do not add any seam allowance to the zipper tabs;
add 3 cm [1¼"] seam allowance to the batting and
lining; use a 1.2 - 1.5 cm [½" - ⅝"] wide bias binding for the stem appliqué; add 0.3 - 0.5 cm [⅛" - ¼"]
seam allowance to all appliqués other than the stem;
add 0.7 cm [¼"] for pieces A and B.

❧ Directions
1 Trace the appliqué design onto piece A. Trace and cut out the appliqué pieces. Appliqué, and embroider to make the pouch top. Sew both the appliquéd piece A and the plain piece A on either side of piece B; press the seams toward piece B. With wrong sides together and batting in between, baste, then quilt the pouch top and the lining (Diagram 1).
2 Using the 3.5 cm [1⅜"] bias binding, bind the pouch openings (Diagram 2). Bringing the bound edges together, sew the zipper to either side of the binding using a backstitch (Diagram 3).
3 Baste the linen ribbon in place on the sides of the pouch (Diagram 4). With right sides together, fold the pouch in half (with zipper partially open); sew the side seams. Trim the seam allowance down to 0.7 cm [¼"], except for one side of the lining. Use the lining fabric to bind the side seam allowances (Diagram 5).
4 Sew the bottom of the bag to create a gusset and bind the raw seam allowance (Diagram 6).
5 To finish the ends of the zipper, bind the zipper ends with the zipper tabs; blindstitch down to cover the ends (Diagram 7).
6 Turn the pouch right side out. Make and attach the zipper pull to the zipper clasp to finish the pouch (Diagram 8).

Diagram 1

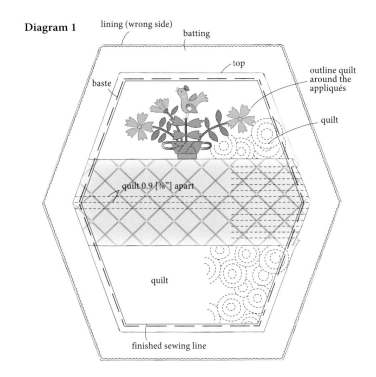

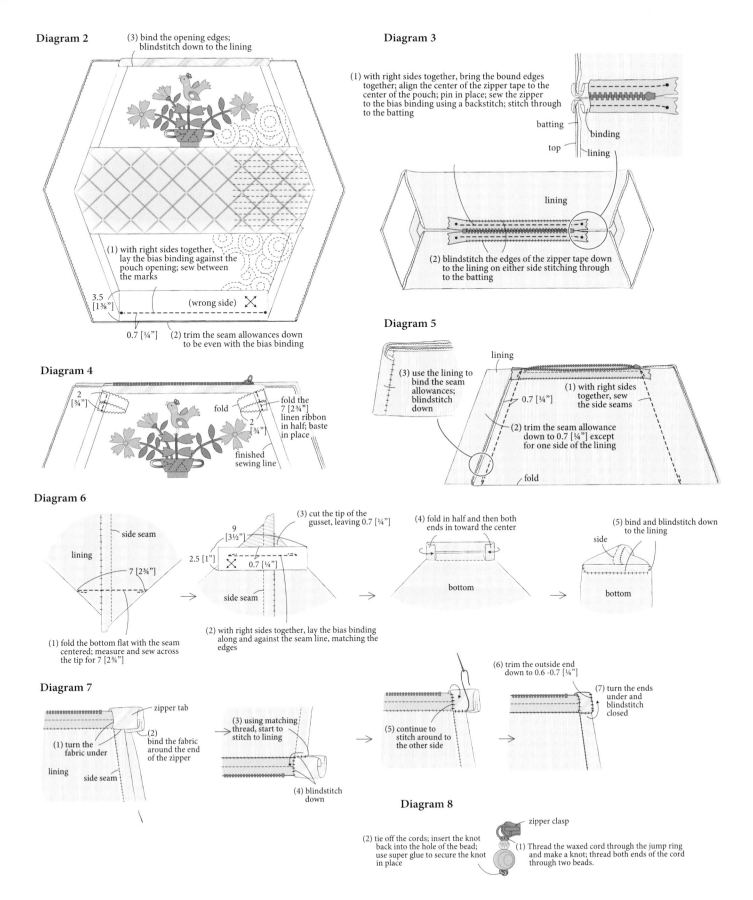

Diagram 2

(3) bind the opening edges; blindstitch down to the lining

(1) with right sides together, lay the bias binding against the pouch opening; sew between the marks

3.5 [1⅜"]

(wrong side) ✕

0.7 [¼"]   (2) trim the seam allowances down to be even with the bias binding

Diagram 3

(1) with right sides together, bring the bound edges together; align the center of the zipper tape to the center of the pouch; pin in place; sew the zipper to the bias binding using a backstitch; stitch through to the batting

batting
binding
top
lining

lining

(2) blindstitch the edges of the zipper tape down to the lining on either side stitching through to the batting

Diagram 4

2 [¾"]   fold   fold the 7 [2¾"] linen ribbon in half; baste in place

2 [¾"]

finished sewing line

Diagram 5

lining

(3) use the lining to bind the seam allowances; blindstitch down

(1) with right sides together, sew the side seams

0.7 [¼"]

(2) trim the seam allowance down to 0.7 [¼"] except for one side of the lining

fold

Diagram 6

side seam

lining

7 [2¾"]

(1) fold the bottom flat with the seam centered; measure and sew across the tip for 7 [2¾"]

9 [3½"]

(3) cut the tip of the gusset, leaving 0.7 [¼"]

2.5 [1"]   ✕   0.7 [¼"]

side seam

(2) with right sides together, lay the bias binding along and against the seam line, matching the edges

(4) fold in half and then both ends in toward the center

bottom

(5) bind and blindstitch down to the lining

side

bottom

Diagram 7

zipper tab

(1) turn the fabric under

(2) bind the fabric around the end of the zipper

lining

side seam

(3) using matching thread, start to stitch to lining

(4) blindstitch down

(5) continue to stitch around to the other side

(6) trim the outside end down to 0.6 -0.7 [¼"]

(7) turn the ends under and blindstitch closed

Diagram 8

zipper clasp

(2) tie off the cords; insert the knot back into the hole of the bead; use super glue to secure the knot in place

(1) Thread the waxed cord through the jump ring and make a knot; thread both ends of the cord through two beads.

99

✳The full-size template/pattern can be found on Side C of the pattern sheet inserts.

⚜ Materials

Lt beige homespun - 22 × 36 cm [8⅝" × 14⅛"] (piece A)
Grey print - 17 × 45 cm [6" × 17¾"] (pieces B, B', E, and E')
Lt beige print - 25 × 11 cm [9¾" × 4⅜"] (piece D)
Assorted fat quarters or scraps - (piecing, appliqué, handle)
Brown homespun - 110 × 35 cm [43¼" × 13¾"] (lining, bias binding)
Batting - 90 × 31 cm [35⅜" × 12¼"]
Interfacing - 2 × 9 cm [¾" × 3½"] (handle)
Embroidery floss - yellow, lt green, green, lt brown

⚜ Finished measurements

19 × 25 cm [7½" × 9¾"]
10 cm [4"] (gusset width)

⚜ Directions

1 Cut out the pattern pieces referring to the dimensional diagram and pattern sheet inserts for piece A of the tea cozy; trace the appliqué design onto it. Trace and cut out the appliqué pieces. Appliqué, and embroider piece A. Sew B to either side of piece A and piece C to the bottom to complete one side. Repeat to make the other side.

2 Appliqué and embroider the gusset (piece D). Sew E to either side of piece D and piece F to the bottom to complete one side. Embroider the rest of motifs and appliqué the leaves over the seams. Repeat to make the other side.

3 For each of the four pieces and with wrong sides together, layer the top and lining with the batting in between; baste, then quilt (Diagram 1).

4 With right sides together, sew one of the gusset pieces to the left of one side of the tea cozy (Diagram 2). Trim the seam allowances to 0.7 cm [¼"], except for the gusset lining and the lower edges. Use the lining to bind the side seams (Diagram 3). Repeat for the other side to make two.

5 With right sides together, sew the pieces together around the curved top edge, leaving the bottom open. Use the same brown homespun as the lining to make a 2.5 × 55 cm [1" × 21⅝"] wide bias binding. Bind the seam allowance (Diagrams 4 & 5). Turn right side out.

6 Use the same brown homespun as the lining to make 2.5 × 80 cm [1" × 31½"] long bias binding. Bind the bottom edge opening of the tea cozy (Diagram 6).

7 Refer to Diagram 7 to make the handle; sew the handle to the top center of the tea cozy to finish (Diagram 8).

Dimensional Diagram

Tea Cozy Front & Back (2 of each)
top (appliquéd piece)
batting
lining (brown homespun)

* Do not add any seam allowance to the interfacing; add 3 cm [1¼"] seam allowance to the batting and lining; use a 1.2 - 1.5 cm [½" - ⅝"] wide bias binding for the stem appliqué; add 0.3 - 0.5 cm [⅛" - ¼"] seam allowance to all appliqués other than the stem; add 0.7 cm [¼"] for the top, lining for the handle and pieces A - F.

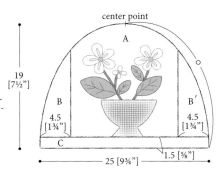

center point

A

19 [7½"]

B   B'

4.5 [1¾"]   4.5 [1¾"]

C

25 [9¾"]   1.5 [⅝"]

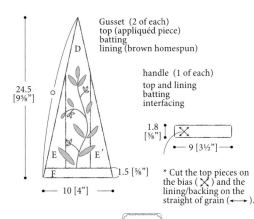

Gusset (2 of each)
top (appliquéd piece)
batting
lining (brown homespun)

D

24.5 [9⅝"]

E   E'

F   1.5 [⅝"]

10 [4"]

handle (1 of each)
top and lining
batting
interfacing

1.8 [⅝"]

9 [3½"]

* Cut the top pieces on the bias (✕) and the lining/backing on the straight of grain (⟷).

Diagram 1

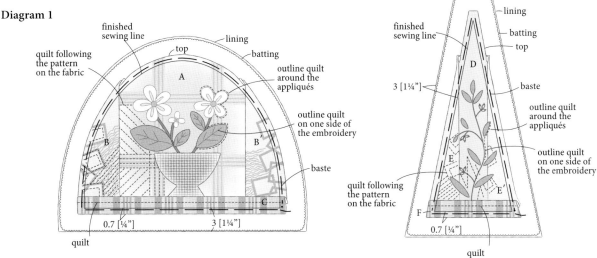

finished sewing line

quilt following the pattern on the fabric

top

lining

batting

A

outline quilt around the appliqués

outline quilt on one side of the embroidery

B   B'

baste

C

0.7 [¼"]   3 [1¼"]

quilt

lining

batting

top

finished sewing line

3 [1¼"]

D

baste

outline quilt around the appliqués

E   E'

outline quilt on one side of the embroidery

quilt following the pattern on the fabric

F

0.7 [¼"]

quilt

Diagram 2

(1) with right sides together, pin the gusset to one side of the tea cozy; sew from one end to the other

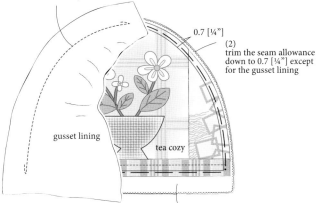

0.7 [¼"]

(2) trim the seam allowance down to 0.7 [¼"] except for the gusset lining

gusset lining

tea cozy

do not trim the seam allowance on the lower edge

Diagram 3

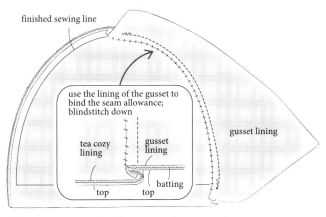

finished sewing line

use the lining of the gusset to bind the seam allowance; blindstitch down

tea cozy lining

gusset lining

gusset lining

batting

top

top

repeat for the other side of the tea cozy to have two similar sections

Diagram 4

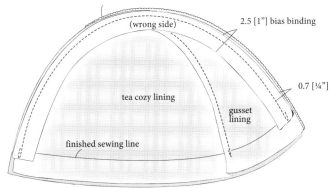

(2) trim away excess lining and batting to match the edge of the bias binding

(wrong side)

2.5 [1"] bias binding

0.7 [¼"]

tea cozy lining

gusset lining

finished sewing line

(1) with right sides together, sew the front and back of the tea cozy together, stitching all the way around the curve and leaving the bottom edge open; with right sides together, pin the bias binding to the curved edge; sew; use the bias binding to bind the seam and blindstitch down to the lining

Diagram 5

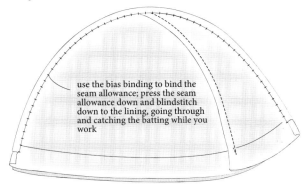

use the bias binding to bind the seam allowance; press the seam allowance down and blindstitch down to the lining, going through and catching the batting while you work

Diagram 7

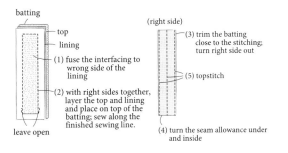

batting

top

lining

(right side)

(1) fuse the interfacing to wrong side of the lining

(3) trim the batting close to the stitching; turn right side out

(2) with right sides together, layer the top and lining and place on top of the batting; sew along the finished sewing line.

(5) topstitch

(4) turn the seam allowance under and inside

leave open

Diagram 6

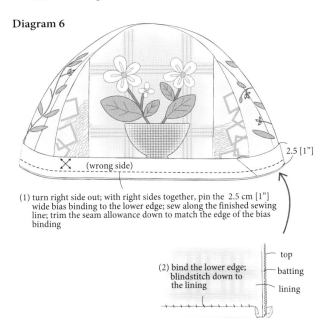

(wrong side)

2.5 [1"]

(1) turn right side out; with right sides together, pin the 2.5 cm [1"] wide bias binding to the lower edge; sew along the finished sewing line; trim the seam allowance down to match the edge of the bias binding

(2) bind the lower edge; blindstitch down to the lining

top

batting

lining

Diagram 8

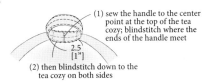

(1) sew the handle to the center point at the top of the tea cozy; blindstitch where the ends of the handle meet

2.5 [1"]

(2) then blindstitch down to the tea cozy on both sides

Tulip Sewing Basket ∗A half-size template/pattern can be found on Side C of the pattern sheet inserts.

🌿 Materials

Lt beige print - 25 × 55 cm [9¾" × 21⅝"] (basket sides top/outer)

Beige homespun - 22 × 50 cm [8⅝" × 19¾"] (handle loops, basket bottom top/outer, bottom strips)

Grey homespun - 40 × 55 cm [15¾" × 21⅝"] (lining, partition)

Muslin - 37 × 42 cm [14½" × 16½"] (facing)

Assorted fat quarters or scraps - (appliqué)

Batting - 37 × 42 cm [14½" × 16½"]

Fusible batting - 31 × 50 cm [12¼" × 19¾"]

Embroidery floss - white, black, green, yellow

Clear template plastic - 25 × 50 cm [9¾" × 19¾"]

Handles (wooden) - 1 pair

Lt beige pom pom trim - 95 cm [37⅜"] long

🌿 Finished measurements
8.6 × 14 cm [3⅜" × 5½"]
11 cm [4⅜"] (height)

🌿 Directions

1 Cut out the pattern pieces referring to the dimensional diagram and pattern sheet inserts for the basket; trace the appliqué design. Trace and cut out the appliqué pieces. Appliqué to each of the sides top pieces (sides A, B, C, D). Sew the side pieces to the bottom piece to create the shape below.

2 Cut out the facing in one piece the same size as the piece above. Layer the appliquéd top and facing fabric with the batting in between; baste. Quilt the sides as desired.

3 Cut out the lining fabric with specified seam allowances and iron the fusible batting to the wrong side (Diagram 1). With right sides together, layer the appliquéd/quilted top and the lining; draw finished sewing lines on the lining and machine sew together the "v" areas. Do not sew along the outside edges of sides (Diagram 2). Measure the bottom and the four sides and cut out the clear template plastic pieces.

4 Trim the seam allowance; clipping into the inner corners, turn right side out and press; machine sew three sides of the bottom; insert the bottom template plastic (Diagram 3).

5 Hand sew the remaining side to secure the bottom template plastic piece in place. Insert each piece into the designated sides. Fold the seam allowances to the inside, sandwich the pom pom trim between the top and lining and stitch closed on each side (Diagram 4).

6 Make the partition (Diagram 5). Make the handle loops and thread them through the holes in the handle (Diagram 6). Insert the edges of the handle loops into the opening of the partition; sew the opening together by sandwiching the pompom trim in between (Diagram 7).

7 Sew the partition to the center point of the basket bottom with stitches at either end (Diagram 8).

8 Lift up the sides and sew the edges together using a ladder stitch. Sew the upper corners of the partition to the basket sides at the center point to finish (Diagram 9).

Dimensional Diagram

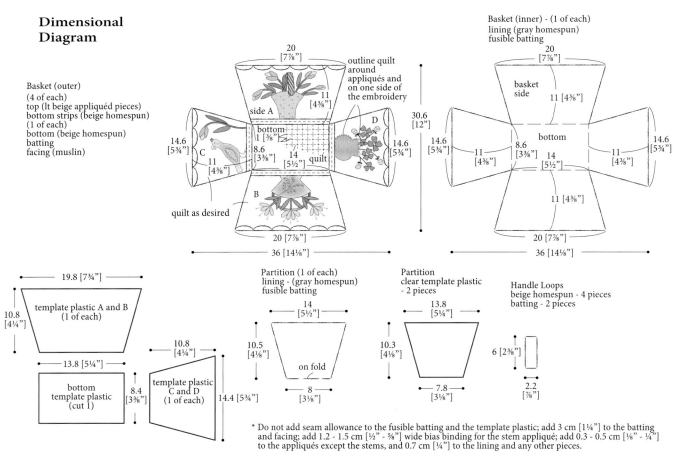

Basket (outer)
(4 of each)
top (lt beige appliquéd pieces)
bottom strips (beige homespun)
(1 of each)
bottom (beige homespun)
batting
facing (muslin)

Basket (inner) - (1 of each)
lining (gray homespun)
fusible batting

Partition (1 of each)
lining - (gray homespun)
fusible batting

Partition
clear template plastic
- 2 pieces

Handle Loops
beige homespun - 4 pieces
batting - 2 pieces

* Do not add seam allowance to the fusible batting and the template plastic; add 3 cm [1¼"] to the batting and facing; add 1.2 - 1.5 cm [½" - ⅝"] wide bias binding for the stem appliqué; add 0.3 - 0.5 cm [⅛" - ¼"] to the appliqués except the stems, and 0.7 cm [¼"] to the lining and any other pieces.

102

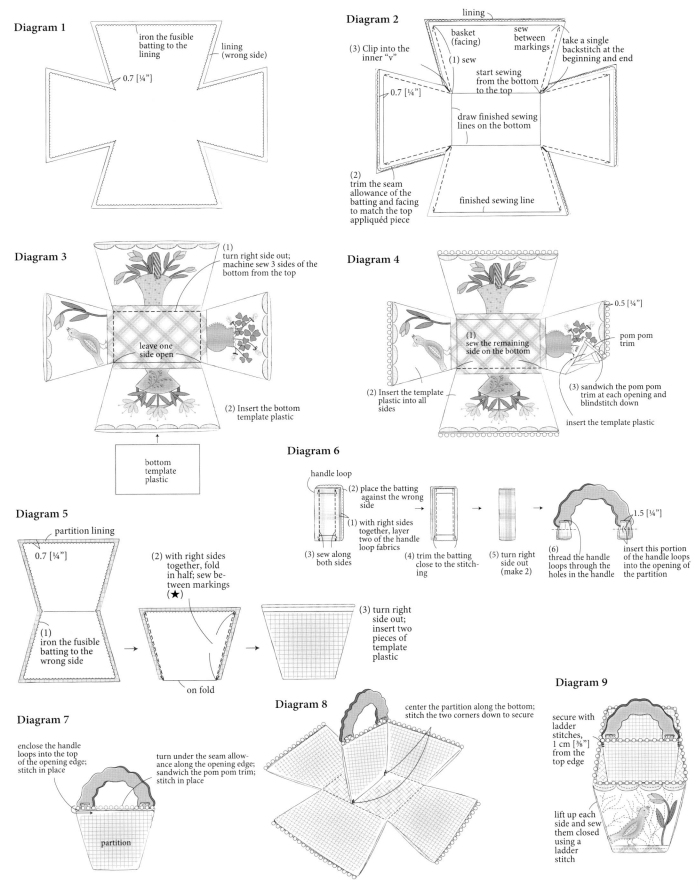

Diagram 1

iron the fusible batting to the lining

lining (wrong side)

0.7 [¼"]

Diagram 2

lining

basket (facing)

sew between markings

take a single backstitch at the beginning and end

(3) Clip into the inner "v"

(1) sew

start sewing from the bottom to the top

draw finished sewing lines on the bottom

0.7 [¼"]

(2) trim the seam allowance of the batting and facing to match the top appliquéd piece

finished sewing line

Diagram 3

(1) turn right side out; machine sew 3 sides of the bottom from the top

leave one side open

(2) Insert the bottom template plastic

bottom template plastic

Diagram 4

0.5 [¼"]

(1) sew the remaining side on the bottom

pom pom trim

(2) Insert the template plastic into all sides

(3) sandwich the pom pom trim at each opening and blindstitch down

insert the template plastic

Diagram 6

handle loop

(2) place the batting against the wrong side

(1) with right sides together, layer two of the handle loop fabrics

(3) sew along both sides

(4) trim the batting close to the stitching

(5) turn right side out (make 2)

(6) thread the handle loops through the holes in the handle

1.5 [¼"]

insert this portion of the handle loops into the opening of the partition

Diagram 5

partition lining

0.7 [¼"]

(1) iron the fusible batting to the wrong side

(2) with right sides together, fold in half; sew between markings (★)

on fold

(3) turn right side out; insert two pieces of template plastic

Diagram 7

enclose the handle loops into the top of the opening edge; stitch in place

turn under the seam allowance along the opening edge; sandwich the pom pom trim; stitch in place

partition

Diagram 8

center the partition along the bottom; stitch the two corners down to secure

Diagram 9

secure with ladder stitches, 1 cm [⅜"] from the top edge

lift up each side and sew them closed using a ladder stitch

Appliquéd Eco-Bag ∗ The full-size template/pattern of the pocket can be found on Side C of the pattern sheet inserts.

❧ **Materials**

Lt beige print - 110 × 42 cm [43¼" × 16½"] (bag body top, handles)
Grey print - 110 × 42 cm [43¼" × 16½"] (lining)
Beige homespun - 25 × 46 cm [9¾" × 18⅛"] (pocket)
Assorted fat quarters or scraps - (appliqués)
Embroidery floss - lt beige, green

❧ **Directions**

1 Cut out the pattern pieces referring to the dimensional diagram and pattern sheet inserts for the bag; trace the appliqué design. Add the appliqué to the right side of the pocket fabric.
2 With right sides together, fold the pocket in half and sew around the edges, leaving an opening for turning right side out. Turn the pocket right side out through the opening; fold the seam allowance inside; press. Topstitch the opening by sewing machine (Diagram 1).
3 Make the handles (Diagram 2).
4 Sew the pocket to the right side of the bag body top. With right sides together, fold the bag body in half; sew the sides seams to make a bag. Turn right side out. Baste the handles to the opening of the top fabric as shown (Diagram 3).
5 With right sides together, fold the bag lining in half; sew the side seams leaving an opening for turning right side out; turn right side out; press. With right sides together, insert the bag lining in the appliquéd bag top; sew around the bag opening at the top edge (Diagram 4).
6 Turn the bag right side out through the opening in the lining so that the lining is on the outside while you are working; tuck the seam allowance inside the lining; finger press; blindstitch closed. Turn the bag right side out. Topstitch around opening by machine to finish (Diagram 5).

❧ Finished measurements
40 × 40 cm [15¾" × 15¾"]

Dimensional Diagram

Bag (1 of each)
top (lt beige print)
lining (gray print)

Handle (cut 4)
(lt beige print)

10.5 [4⅛"]   handle position
15 [5⅞"]

bag body and lining

appliqué

pocket
(beige homespun)
1 piece

40 [15¾"]   38 [15"]

leave open   12 [4¾"]   leave open

8 [3⅛"]

22 [8⅝"]

5 [2"]   on fold

10 [4"]   on fold

22 [8⅝"]   5.5 [2⅛"]   9 [3½"]

40 [15¾"]

2 [¾"]

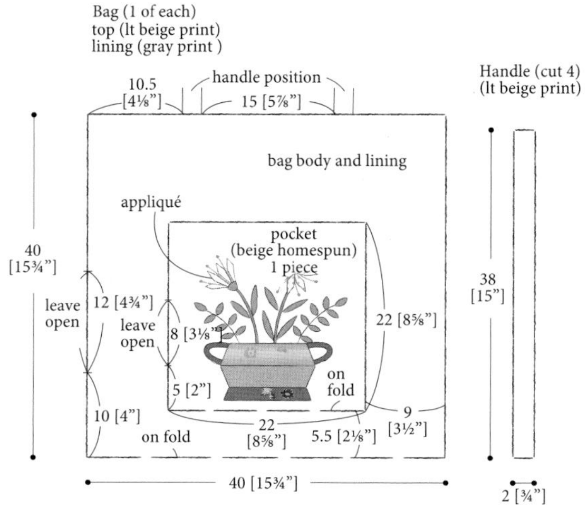

* Use a 1.2 - 1.5 cm [½" - ⅝"] wide bias binding for the stem appliqué; add 0.3 - 0.5 cm [⅛" - ¼"] seam allowance to all appliqués other than the stem; add 0.7 cm [¼"] for all other pieces.

Diagram 1

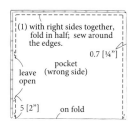

(1) with right sides together, fold in half; sew around the edges

pocket (wrong side)

0.7 [¼"]

leave open

5 [2"]   on fold

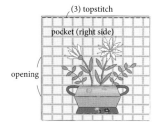

(3) topstitch

pocket (right side)

opening

(2) turn right side out; fold seam allowances under; blindstitch opening closed

Diagram 2

handle (wrong side)

→   topstitch

0.7 [¼"]   2 [¾"]   0.7 [¼"]

(1) with right sides together, layer two handle pieces; sew along the long sides

(2) turn right side out; topstitch on both long sides (make 2)

Diagram 3

(3) baste the handles just outside the finished sewing line within the seam allowance

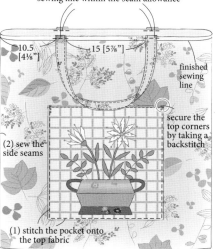

10.5 [4⅛"]   15 [5⅞"]

finished sewing line

secure the top corners by taking a backstitch

(2) sew the side seams

(1) stitch the pocket onto the top fabric

Diagram 4

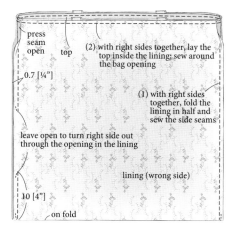

press seam open   top

0.7 [¼"]

(2) with right sides together, lay the top inside the lining; sew around the bag opening

(1) with right sides together, fold the lining in half and sew the side seams

leave open to turn right side out through the opening in the lining

lining (wrong side)

10 [4"]

on fold

Diagram 5

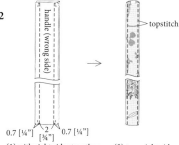

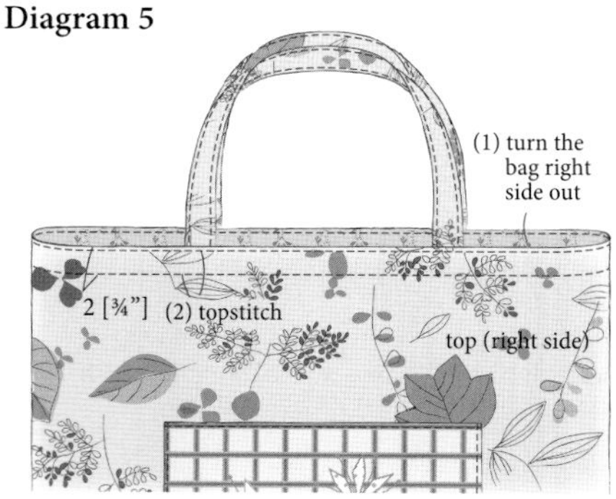

(1) turn the bag right side out

2 [¾"]   (2) topstitch

top (right side)

Shown on p. 49

Floral Bird Tote

*A half-size template/pattern can be found on Side D of the pattern sheet inserts.

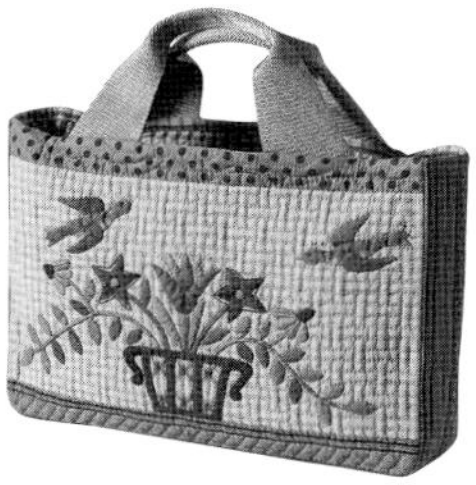

Finished measurements

28 × 40 cm [11" × 15¾"]; 9 cm [3½"] (gusset width)

Materials

Lt blue homespun - 23 × 42 cm [9" × 16½"] (bag body front)
Lt brown homespun - 110 × 42 cm [43¼" × 16½"] (bag body back, piece B, gusset)
Polka dot print - 5 × 42 cm [2" × 16½"] (piece A)
Beige homespun - 110 × 85 cm [43¼" × 33½"] (bag lining, gusset lining, bias binding)
Assorted fat quarters or scraps - (piecing, appliqués)
Batting - 100 × 50 cm [39⅜" × 19¾"]
Heavyweight fusible interfacing - 9 × 92 cm [3½" × 36¼"]
Grey nylon webbing - 7 × 76 cm [2¾" × 29⅞"] (handles)
Embroidery floss - brown, lt beige, yellow, black

Directions

1 Add appliqués to the appliqué background fabric. Sew piece A to the upper edge and piece B to the lower edge, to make the top of the bag front. With wrong sides together and batting in between, layer the top and lining; baste, then quilt.

2 Cut the bag back as a single piece, then with wrong sides together and batting in between, layer the top and lining; baste, then quilt as shown or as desired.

3 Make the gusset (Diagram 1).

4 With right sides together, sew the gusset and bag front together. Trim the seam allowances down to 0.7 cm [¼"] except for the lining and at the bag opening. Use the lining to bind the seam allowance; press toward the bag; blindstitch down (Diagram 2). Repeat to sew the bag back to the gusset.

5 Make two handles (Diagram 3). Turn the bag body right side out. With right sides together, place handles in position at the bag opening; baste them just outside the finished sewing line (Diagram 4).

6 Make the 3 × 105 cm [1¼" ×41⅜"] bias binding out of the beige homespun. With right sides together, lay it against the bag opening; sew along the finished sewing line. Trim the excess seam allowance along the bag opening edge (Diagram 4). Use the bias binding to bind the seam allowance and blindstitch down to the lining to finish (Diagram 5).

Dimensional Diagram

Bag Body Front (1 of each)
top (appliquéd piece)
batting
lining (beige homespun)

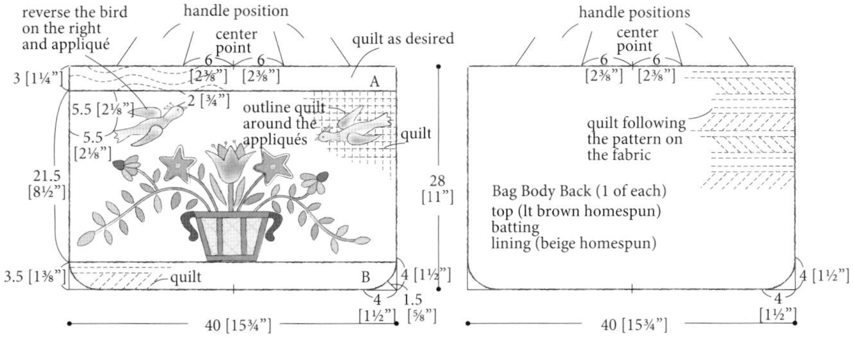
reverse the bird on the right and appliqué
handle position
center point
quilt as desired
6
6
[2⅜"]
[2⅜"]
3 [1¼"]
A
5.5 [2⅛"]
2 [¾"]
outline quilt around the appliqués
5.5 [2⅛"]
quilt
21.5 [8½"]
28 [11"]
3.5 [1⅜"]
quilt
B
4 [1½"]
4 [1½"]
1.5 [⅝"]
40 [15¾"]
handle positions
center point
6
6
[2⅜"]
[2⅜"]
quilt following the pattern on the fabric
Bag Body Back (1 of each)
top (lt brown homespun)
batting
lining (beige homespun)
4 [1½"]
4 [1½"]
40 [15¾"]

Gusset (1 of each)
top (lt brown homespun) • lining (beige homespun)
heavyweight fusible interfacing • batting

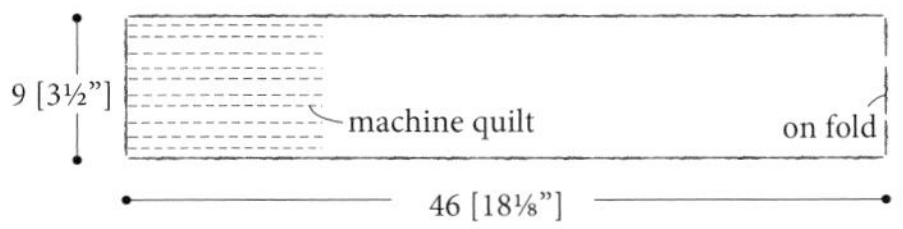
9 [3½"]
machine quilt
on fold
46 [18⅛"]

* Do not add any seam allowance to the interfacing; add 3 cm [1¼"] seam allowance to the batting and lining; use a 1.2 - 1.5 cm [½" - ⅝"] wide bias binding for the stem appliqué; add 0.3 - 0.5 cm [⅛" - ¼"] seam allowance to all appliqués other than the stem; add 0.7 cm [¼"] for all else.

Diagram 1

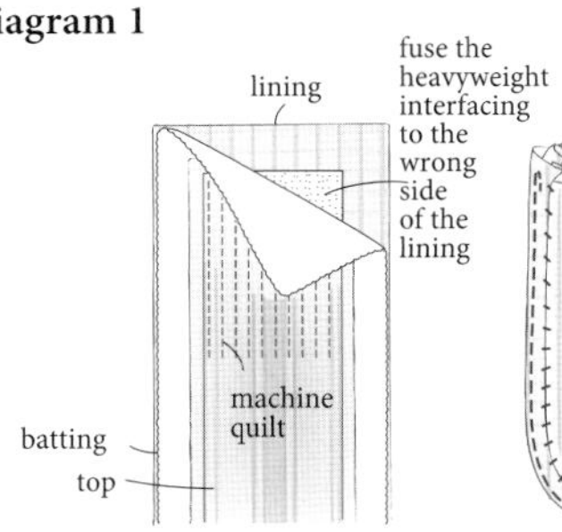
lining
fuse the heavyweight interfacing to the wrong side of the lining
machine quilt
batting
top

Diagram 2

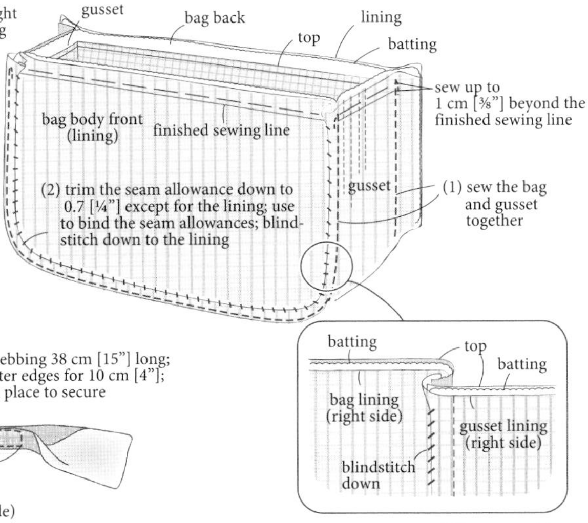
gusset
bag back
top
lining
batting
sew up to 1 cm [⅜"] beyond the finished sewing line
bag body front (lining)
finished sewing line
gusset
(1) sew the bag and gusset together
(2) trim the seam allowance down to 0.7 [¼"] except for the lining; use to bind the seam allowances; blind-stitch down to the lining
batting
top
batting
bag lining (right side)
gusset lining (right side)
blindstitch down

Diagram 3

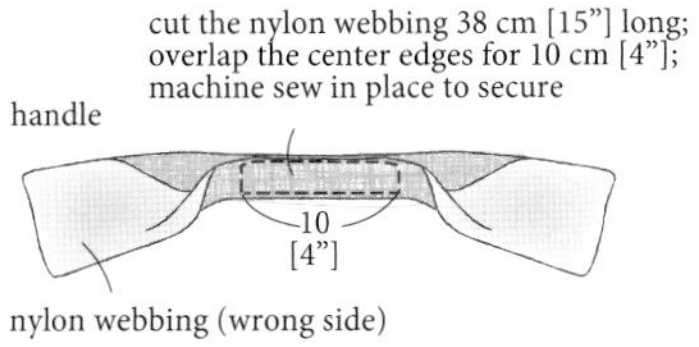
cut the nylon webbing 38 cm [15"] long; overlap the center edges for 10 cm [4"]; machine sew in place to secure
handle
10 [4"]
nylon webbing (wrong side)

Diagram 4

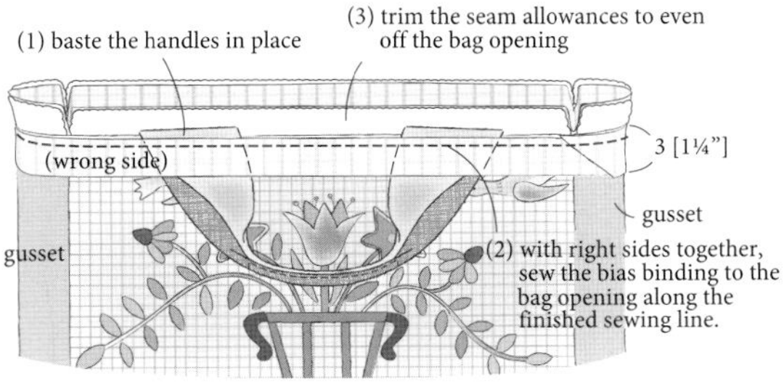
(1) baste the handles in place
(3) trim the seam allowances to even off the bag opening
(wrong side)
3 [1¼"]
gusset
gusset
(2) with right sides together, sew the bias binding to the bag opening along the finished sewing line.

Diagram 5

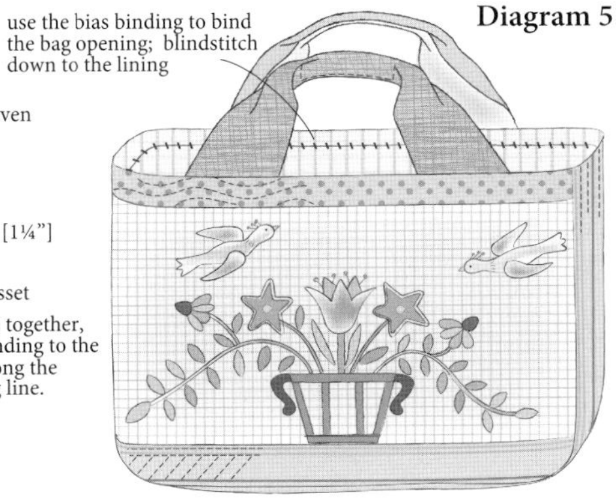
use the bias binding to bind the bag opening; blindstitch down to the lining

Vases of Flowers Wall Quilt ＊A half-size template/pattern can be found on Side D of the pattern sheet inserts.

🌿 Finished measurements
141.4 × 156.4 cm [55⅝" × 61¼"]

Wall Quilt (1 of each)
top (appliqués and piecework)
batting
backing (beige homespun)

Dimensional Diagram

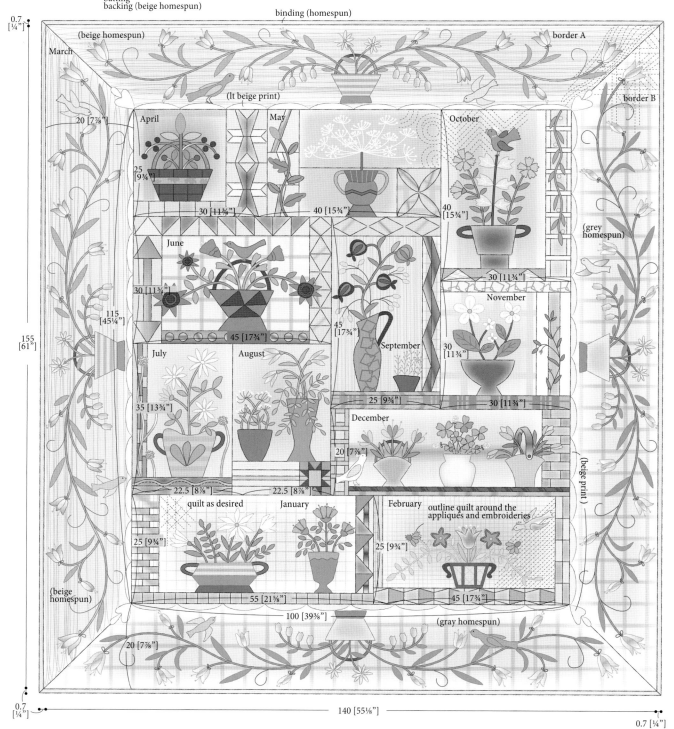

binding (homespun)

0.7 [¼"]

(beige homespun)

border A

March

border B

20 [7⅞"]

(lt beige print)

April

May

October

(grey homespun)

25 [9¾"]

30 [11¾"]

40 [15¾"]

40 [15¾"]

June

115 [45¼"]

155 [61"]

30 [11¾"]

30 [11¾"]

45 [17¾"]

September

November

45 [17¾"]

30 [11¾"]

July

August

25 [9¾"]

30 [11¾"]

35 [13¾"]

December

20 [7⅞"]

(beige print)

22.5 [8⅞"]

22.5 [8⅞"]

quilt as desired

January

February

outline quilt around the appliqués and embroideries

25 [9¾"]

25 [9¾"]

(beige homespun)

55 [21⅝"]

45 [17¾"]

100 [39⅜"]

(gray homespun)

20 [7⅞"]

0.7 [¼"]

140 [55⅛"]

0.7 [¼"]

* Add 1 cm [⅜"] to the borders; 5 cm [2"] to the backing and batting; use a 1.2 - 1.5 cm [½" - ⅝"] wide bias binding for the stem appliqué; add 0.3 - 0.5 cm [⅛" - ¼"] seam allowance to all appliqués other than the stem; add 0.7 cm [¼"] for all else.

Materials

Assorted fat quarters or scraps - (piecing, appliqués, appliqué background blocks)

Lt beige print (use the wrong side of a fabric as the right side) - 23 × 50 cm [9" × 19¾"] (scalloped edge, appliqués)

Beige print - 23 × 50 cm [9" × 19¾"] (scalloped edge, appliqués)

Beige homespun - 157 × 44 cm [61¾" × 17¼"] (borders A & B)

Grey homespun - 157 × 44 cm [61¾" × 17¼"] (borders A & B)

Beige homespun - 110 × 300 cm [43¼" × 118"](backing)

Beige and brown homespun - 110 × 70 cm [43¼" × 27½"] (bias binding)

Batting - 165 × 150 cm [65" × 59"]

Embroidery floss - several colors of your choice in required amount

1. Making the Top

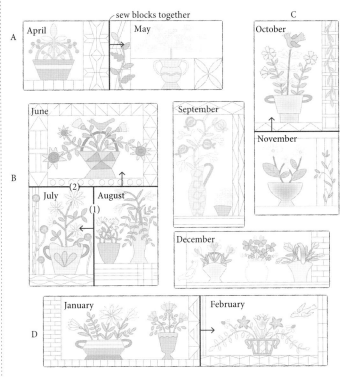

1 To make the quilt center, refer to the pattern sheet inserts and the Dimensional Diagram to find and make the 11 pieced, appliquéd and embroidered blocks. When sewing the individual blocks together, follow the diagram above to make 4 sections (A to D). Press the seam allowances in the directions marked by the arrows above.

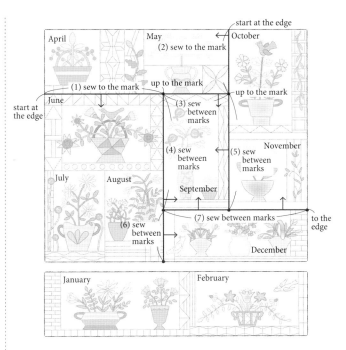

2 Following the (1) through (7) order specified in the diagram above, sew sections A, B, and C together along with the September and December blocks. Next, sew this larger piece to section D, sewing from edge to edge; press the seam allowance toward the larger section. This completes the center of the quilt.

border A

border B

starting mark for mitered corners

sew between marks

sew between the marks

to the mitered corner edge

3 To make borders A and B, referring to the pattern sheet inserts and Dimensional Diagrams, appliqué and embroider the top fabric. With right sides together and matching edges, sew the two borders A to the top and bottom of the quilt center between the marks (0.7 cm [¼"] in from each edge). Next, with right sides together, sew the two borders B to the quilt center between marks. To miter the corner, start at one corner; with right sides together, pin between the marks at the inside border to the outer corner. Sew from the mark out to the outer corner using a 0.7 cm [¼"] seam allowance. Repeat for each corner. Press the seam allowance toward the direction marked by an arrow in the diagram above.

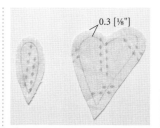

0.3 [⅛"]

blindstitch

4 To finish the quilt top, appliqué the four hearts on the inner corners of the border. Trace the appliqué design on the right side of the fabric. Cut out the appliqué patterns, adding a 0.3 cm [⅛"] seam allowance. Stitch down; repeat to complete four corners.

✐ **Layering and Basting the Quilt**

Make the backing and batting (165 × 150 cm [65" × 59"]) by referring to the Dimensional Diagram. Smooth out the backing fabric (wrong side up) on the floor or flat surface; use thumbtacks, pins or tape at the four corners and along the edges to hold it taut. Lay the batting on top of the backing; re-tack, re-pin or use the tape to also hold the batting taut. Center the quilt top on top of the layers. Re-tack, re-pin or use the tape again around the edges of the quilt top. Start in the center of the quilt top and baste out to the edges.

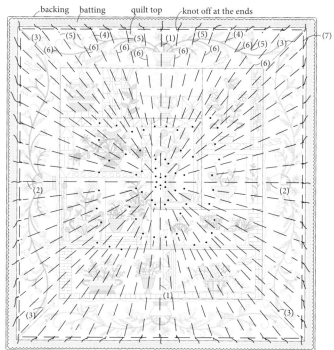

backing   batting   quilt top   knot off at the ends

(3) (5) (4) (5) (1) (5) (4) (5) (3) (7)
(6) (6) (6) (6) (6) (6) (6)
(6)

(2)   (2)

(1)

(3)   (3)

Basting Order
- center vertical lines (1), center horizontal lines (2), diagonal lines (3), areas between the center and the diagonal lines (4), areas between the lines made previously (5), areas between the lines made previously (6), and around the entire edge of the quilt (7)

3. Loading the Quilt onto a Quilting Frame and Quilting the Quilt

* A quilting frame is not required. If you do not have a quilting frame, you can use a quilting hoop or choose another method for quilting a large piece.

use thumbtacks to secure the fabric leader to the wood
roller bar
fold
fabric leader
approximately 10 cm [4"]

1 Attach a very strong fabric (such as canvas) to the frame, using thumbtacks to secure it to the roller bar. Repeat for the other roller bar. These become the leaders of the frame, to which you attach your quilt sandwich.

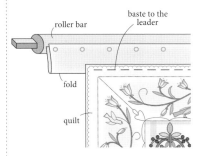
roller bar
baste to the leader
fold
quilt

2 Align and center the edge of the quilt sandwich on the fabric leader; baste to the leader. Making sure that the quilt is laying straight, repeat this by attaching the opposite end of the quilt to the other leader.

3 Having someone help you, roll the quilt over the roller bars from both sides so that the very center of the quilt is showing between the bars. Make sure that the quilt sandwich does not have any wrinkles in it as you roll.

Marking the Quilt
Quilting lines are typically drawn on the quilt top prior to putting the quilt sandwich layers together. For this project, you will draw quilting lines on the quilt sandwich after it is loaded onto the quilting frame or hoop. Draw the quilting lines as desired as you go. If you want to draw lines on an angle or crosshatch patterns, use a ruler for accuracy. If following the patterns on the fabric or quilting flowing lines, quilt freehand without adding any marks.

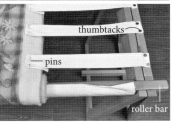
thumbtacks
pins
roller bar

4 Insert the roller bars into the grooves on the quilting frame. Make eight smaller fabric leaders, 5 × 20 cm [2" × 7⅞"] for the sides. Secure the ends to the wood of the quilt frame with thumbtacks at equal intervals (four on each side). Pin the side edges of the quilt sandwich to these side leaders so that the quilt stays taut in the frame.

5 Find a chair or stool that will position you at a comfortable height as you lean over the quilting frame. Thread a quilting between needle with the color that you desire. I usually pick a color that will blend in well with the color of fabric I am working on. Begin to quilt from the center and work your way out by quilting the background, followed by quilting inside each appliqué. Then, outline quilt around each appliqué and embroidery. You should try to take approximately 3 stitches in 1 cm [⅜"]. It is ideal to have the same size stitches showing on both the front and back of your work. Once you have completed quilting the center section, remove the side leader pins and roll the quilt to move on to the next section to quilt. Put it back in the quilting frame, re-pin and continue to quilt.

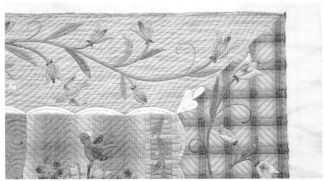

6 When you've completed quilting the entire top, remove the quilted sandwich; remove the basting stitches except those around the perimeter.

4. Cutting the Bias Strips for the Binding

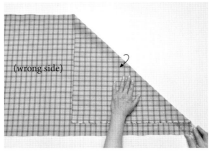

1 Lay fabric on a marking/cutting surface and fold down at an angle, using the markings on your ruler to achieve a perfect 45° angle. Carefully fold the fabric back up, keeping the ruler at a 45° angle. Using a chalk pencil, draw the first marking line that will be used as a reference line.

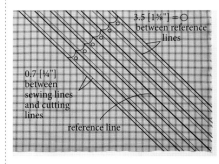

2 Draw the cutting lines at 3.5 cm [1⅜"] intervals from the reference line. Draw the sewing lines 0.7 cm [¼"] away from each of the cutting lines. You might prefer to use different color chalk pencils to easily distinguish the two kinds of markings.

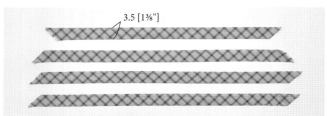

3 Cut the fabric apart on the marked cutting lines to create 3.5 cm [1⅜"] wide bias strips.

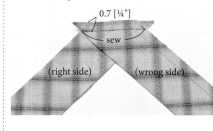

4 Take 2 bias strips and lay them crossed with right sides together, to create right angles. Match the edges. Draw a 0.7 cm [¼"] sewing line to mark the seam allowance. Sew from one end to the other, using a backstitch.

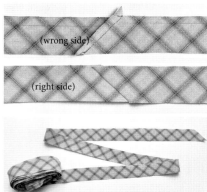

5 Finger-press the seam to one side (or press open if sewn by machine). Trim off the rabbit ears at each seam as you continue to add strips to create continuous bias binding. Sew enough of the strips together to equal approximately 610 cm [240" or 6½ yards].

5. Binding the Quilt

1 Using a marking pencil, draw the finished sewing line on each side of the quilt borders. If the quilting caused shrinkage in comparison to the original dimensions, adjust the finished sewing line to allow a 0.7 cm [¼"] seam allowance. Note that the widths of all borders should be the same.

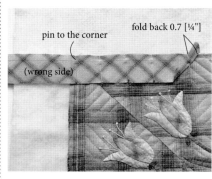

2 Start attaching the binding at the lower right of the quilt where the seams will be the most inconspicuous. With right sides together, place the binding on the quilt, edges together. Match the seam lines marked on the binding and the quilt and pin in place. Folding the end of the binding back 0.7 cm [¼"] at the beginning, pin all the way to the first corner.

3 Using the double backstitch, stitch along the sewing line and stop 0.7 cm [¼"] in from the end. Then backtack to secure the stitches.

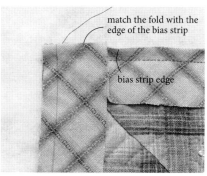

4 Fold the binding up at a 45° angle and then straight back down, laying it along the quilt and matching edges.

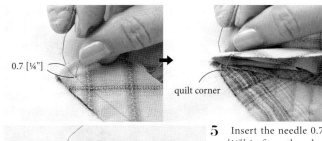

0.7 [¼"]

quilt corner

5 Insert the needle 0.7 cm [¼"] in from the edge or at the same spot where you ended. Using straight pins, pin the binding to the quilt, right sides together all the way to the next corner.

6 Taking the threaded needle, insert it into the corner of the binding to the other side, matching the finished sewing lines.

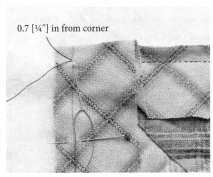

0.7 [¼"] in from corner

7 Push the needle through to the backing and backstitch right at the point where you just brought the needle through to secure the binding at the corner.

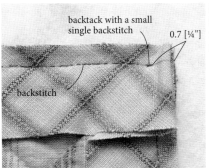

backtack with a small single backstitch

0.7 [¼"]

backstitch

8 Turn the quilt and using a backstitch, continue to sew along the side to the next corner.

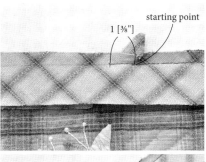

starting point

1 [⅜"]

9 Repeat steps 3 - 8 until you almost reach the starting point, using a backstitch. To finish the binding, overlap the binding over the folded starting point; trim down, so that the overlapping binding is 1 cm [⅜"]. Stitch it down to the end.

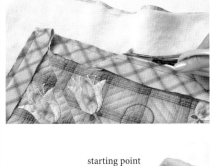

10 Trim the excess seam allowance from the edge of the quilt, so that the backing and batting is even with the edges of top and binding.

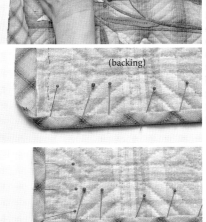

starting point

(backing)

11 Overlap the starting and ending points of the binding. Turn the quilt over and fold the binding from the front to the back. Cover the raw edges and pin the binding in place around the entire quilt. Pin in place. At each corner, fold the binding to create a perfect miter. To complete the quilt, blindstitch the binding down to the backing, catching the batting in the stitches. I do not stitch the miters or the areas where the binding overlaps.

Yoko Saito

A quilter, designer and author of world renown, Yoko Saito learned to quilt after seeing antique quilts on a trip to America. Over the years, she expanded her horizon to also include European and Scandinavian countries in her design work. Her beautiful quilts and quilted works are unique in the use of colors, exquisite designs and intricate quilting and handwork techniques. She teaches quilting at schools and through correspondence courses as well as being on television shows. Her patterns are often published in magazines. She has become increasingly popular among quilters around the world and holds seminars and exhibitions overseas as her schedule allows.

Quilt Party Co., Ltd.
Active Ichikawa 2F
1-23-2, Ichikawa, Ichikawa-shi,
Chiba-Ken, Japan 272-034

http://www.quilt.co.jp (Japanese)
http://shop.quilt.co.jp/en/index.htm (English)

Original Title	Saito Yoko Quilt no Hanataba
Author	Yoko Saito
	©2012 Yoko Saito
First Edition	Originally published in Japan in 2012
Published by:	NHK Publishing, Inc.
	41-1 Udagawa-cho, Shibuya-ku,
	Tokyo, Japan 150-8081
	http://www.nhk-book.co.jp
Translation	©2014 Stitch Publications, LLC
English Translation Rights	arranged with Stitch Publications, LLC through
	Tuttle-Mori Agency, Inc.
Published by:	Stitch Publications, LLC
	P.O. Box 16694
	Seattle, WA 98116
	http://www.stitchpublications.com
Printed & Bound	KHL Printing, Singapore
ISBN	978-0-9859746-7-1
PCN	Library of Congress Control Number: 2014941747

Quilt Party Production   Satomi Funamoto
Kazuko Yamada
Katsumi Mizusawa

Staff
Book Design	Manami Sudo
Photography	Yasuo Nagumo
	Narumi Shimose
Editorial Assistant	Chikami Okuda
Stylist	Terumi Inoue
Illustrations	tinyeggs studio (Yumiko Omori)
Pattern Sheet Illustrations	Factory Water
Copyeditor	Hiroko Yamauchi
Editor	Chiko Onuma (NHK Publishing)

This English edition is published by arrangement with NHK Publishing, Inc., through Tuttle-Mori agency, Inc